The English Curriculum under Fire

What Are the Real Basics?

George Hillocks, Jr., Editor
University of Chicago

National Council of Teachers of English
1111 Kenyon Road, Urbana, Illinois 61801

101404

Book Design: Tom Kovacs

NCTE Stock Number 13982

Library of Congress Cataloging in Publication Data

Main entry under title:

The English curriculum under fire.

    Papers presented at a conference held in 1978 and sponsored by the University of Chicago's Dept. of Education and the Illinois Humanities Council.
    Includes bibliographical references.
    1. English philology—Study and teaching—United States—Congresses. I. Hillocks, George. II. University of Chicago. Dept. of Education. III. Illinois Humanities Council.
PE68.U5E56   1982   428'.007'1073   82-12440
ISBN 0-8141-1398-2

Contents

Introduction

In 1978 when the current wave of attacks on English programs had barely begun, the Department of Education at the University of Chicago asked a number of scholars to come together to consider what is most basic to the study of English in the schools. Out of that invitation came a conference entitled "The English Curriculum under Fire." Today, as the attacks continue with increased intensity, the responses of those scholars have even greater relevance. The following are six of the eight papers presented at that conference.

In the first, George Hillocks, Jr., surveys the nature of the attacks, which range from charges of incompetency to varieties of censorship, and suggests why English teachers may be more vulnerable to public criticism than members of other professions. He urges that English teachers take increased responsibility for what happens in English programs. Basic to such an effort is the kind of thinking exemplified in the papers by Wayne C. Booth, James R. Squire, E. D. Hirsch, Jr., James E. Miller, Jr., and Bruno Bettelheim, each of which considers what is most basic to education in English and the language arts.

Wayne C. Booth addresses the essential question of why we do what we do. He defines rhetoric as the center of the language arts—"the simple matter of learning to understand what people are really saying, learning to look at what words really mean, and learning to respond with words that do important work in the world." He makes clear the need to move beyond using such knowledge merely to detect false rhetoric. Knowledge of rhetoric allows us to create as well as to defend. Words, he argues, have the power to make the present and direct the future: "Our minds and souls have been made mainly out of other people's rhetoric." In examining why we do what we do, Booth takes us through a powerful chain of syllogisms, arguing from the initial premise that "individual freedom is a fundamental value we all pursue, and indeed ought to pursue, as essential to all else that we value" to the final conclusion "that liberal education as the study of rhetoric is our best hope for preserving the possibility of free activity of any kind." Such are the basics to which we must return.

In the third paper, James R. Squire examines the cry for basics in the teaching of writing in light of the "serious questions about the quality and the amount of instruction and practice that children are receiving in writing." He offers four neglected "touchstones," attention to which can improve the teaching of writing. First, schools must increase the time devoted to providing instruction and practice in writing; second, schools must deal with a variety of language functions and require writing to be done across the disciplines—not merely in English and language arts; third, schools must provide time not only for learning such supportive skills as spelling and punctuation but especially for learning the basic processes of composing; and, fourth, he urges that we identify the most teachable moments in the basic composing process and give those priority in teaching. Anyone seriously concerned about structuring or evaluating writing programs in schools will find these guidelines useful.

E. D. Hirsch, Jr., author of the fourth paper, also turns his attention to composition. He first considers the question of why writing is so difficult and posits two major causes of the difficulty. First, writing is decontextualized, written apart from concrete situations and for vaguely defined audiences, and, therefore, requires far greater explicitness than does ordinary speech. Second, writing requires the use of so many skills at once that it often results in "cognitive overload," a condition in which, as the difficulty of the task increases, the writing becomes less and less adequate. Professor Hirsch then offers recommendations for instruction, which include making young writers aware of the differences between writing and speech and reducing the cognitive demands through various strategies. His paper provides useful ideas for teachers and curriculum makers.

The final two papers attend to what is basic in literature and reading. In "The Basics and the Imagination," James E. Miller, Jr., "sifts through the debris" of the past and reviews two of the attempts to get down to basics since the launching of Sputnik: the drive for excellence impelled by curriculum centers sponsored by the United States Office of Education, with their emphasis on highly structured curricula, and the counterforce of the Dartmouth Conference in 1966, with its emphasis on more open "growth" models. Both seemed to produce "basics" worthy of commitment at the time, "basics" which now lie in ruin. Turning to the present, Miller "scans the horizon" for sources of help. He finds university English departments preoccupied with their own declining fortunes, recent literary criticism offering only a kind of egocentric "critical nihilism," and even recent literature similarly "self-centered and of diminishing relevance." His "re-excavation of the foundations" reveals the education of the literary imagination to be an essential basic, basic to morality and under-standing, to growth and awareness.

In the final essay, Bruno Bettelheim, through a fascinating series of examples, illustrates "The Unconscious at Work in Reading." He argues that the unconscious allows children to make reading a deeply personal experience when they invest words with personal meanings. This necessary personalizing of the reading experience sometimes results in what adults regard as misreadings. Bettelheim argues that such errors are simply signs of the child's need to find personal meaning in reading. When adults accept such misreadings and under-stand the needs that precipitated them, children spontaneously correct their own "misreadings."

In each case, the contributors to this volume have cited "basics" that are far different from those of the current "back-to-basics" move-ment, whose basics these scholars regard as at best subskills to be routinized. Perhaps a paraphrase of Wayne Booth's subtitle is a fitting title for this whole collection: "Our Basics Are More Basic Than Your Basics." Our task as English teachers, then, is to emphasize the core of English studies—what all the contributors might agree to call the education and growth of the linguistic imagination.

The conference at which the papers in this volume were presented was sponsored by the University of Chicago's Department of Educa-tion and the Illinois Humanities Council and by grants from Harcourt Brace Jovanovich, Inc.; Harper and Row Publishers, Inc.; Hayden Book Company, Inc.; D. C. Heath and Company; Houghton Mifflin Company; Scholastic Magazines, Inc.; and Time Incorporated. With-out the support of all these groups the conference would not have been possible.

Besides the speakers whose work is included here, a number of other people made important contributions to the success of the conference. These include Janet Emig of Rutgers University and David Thorburn of Massachusetts Institute of Technology, who were both featured speakers but who did not make their work available for this publication. An extremely important facet of the conference were the continuing discussion groups led by prominent figures in the fields of English and education, including Marguerite Bougere, Marjorie Farmer, Stephen M. Judy, Michael Marsden, John C. Mellon, Lee Odell, Roy C. O'Donnell, Walter Petty, Joseph M. Williams, Larry Johannessen, and Michael Smith. The work of Faye Kachur, who assisted in planning the conference from its inception to its completion, was particularly important.

English Programs under Fire

George Hillocks, Jr.
University of Chicago

I first realized how ubiquitous the attacks on English programs were when I encountered a lady in the woods a couple of summers ago. She and her family had camped next to mine. She was something of a behemoth with a bellow to match. When she wanted to communicate with her friends three campsites away, she would simply raise her voice a few decibels to overcome interference from noisy children and rock music. You might say she was a mass medium all by herself. Although I was impressed by this vocal virtuosity, I made no attempt to develop her acquaintance.

For two afternoons I remained at camp alone, writing at a table in the open. This obviously strange behavior piqued her curiosity and, on the second day, she trundled over to investigate. She wasted no words. "I notice," she said, "that you've been sitting there writing, and writing, and writing! You must be a teacher, and I'll bet an English teacher." I opined as how I was, having been caught red-handed at a telltale activity. I might have tried to deny it, had I known what was coming—a harangue thinly disguised as a question.

"What do you think of these English programs in all the high schools nowadays? Why, do you know the kids don't have to take any special courses—no grammar, no writing? And the so-called literature they read in some of them. It's no more than the stuff anybody can pick out of the rack at the corner drugstore. Some of it is downright trashy. These young people are coming through high school, and I know for a fact that they are not learning grammar—or how to write a good sentence. And they don't even read the great writers." She went on to explain, permitting only an occasional "Hmmm" or "Uh-huh" from me, that she had been invited by the principal of the local high school to participate in a citizens' committee charged with evaluating the English program. The principal thought she'd be a pushover and just go along with everything, she said. But she got down to work and

1

did some "research." She obtained the course descriptions to see what was being offered. She talked with personnel managers at several large companies in the area *and* the chair of the English department at a local community college. They all agreed that the students graduating from the local high school couldn't spell, couldn't write a good sentence, and couldn't even read directions for filling out applications very well. She went on at some length about the failures of English programs.

I decided, then and there, that when people get all excited about such things during the summer and out in the woods at that, we are in trouble as English teachers.

Time magazine confirmed my fears a few weeks later. The November 14, 1977, issue carried a cover story, "High Schools under Fire," that did a pretty good job on English teaching as it related the problems confronting American high schools. A little informal content analysis lays it on the line. The article makes about twenty-five specific references to instruction, curricula, or test results in particular subject-matter areas. Sixteen of them are to English or language arts, and all sixteen are perjorative. Some examples may not be altogether gratuitous here. According to *Time,* course titles sound like question categories on television game shows: Great Sleuths, Exploring the Occult, Contemporary Issues. A ninth-grade teacher of college-preparatory English is described as instructing "her students on how to talk to one another. She pouts and gestures to illustrate tone and attitude changes, then reads a short story about being loving and capable. For homework, the students are told to make a tear in a sheet of paper each time someone is mean to them and a pencil mark when someone makes them feel good about themselves." At another high school a sophomore honors English class watches act 3, scene 1, of *The Merchant of Venice* on film. "There is no discussion and only a few questions about the plot. The eighteen students and their teacher all hunch silently in their seats." A student complains that teachers don't give enough practice in writing; another complains that someone "screwed up" because he had not learned grammar. A teacher of German observes that her students can't spell English, and the authors of the article lament declining test scores and the lack of standard survey courses.

I suspect that there has been dissatisfaction with English teaching for some time—even before the days of declining test scores. But the test score data—the verbal SAT score dropped 47 points between 1963 and 1976—has provided all sorts of critics with new weapons and has certainly received public attention. One study published in 1975 surveyed data from several achievement test batteries including the SAT, PSAT, and ACT for college entrance as well as tests used at lower grades: Iowa Tests of Educational Development, Iowa Tests of Basic Skills, Comprehensive Tests of Basic Skills, and National Assessment of Educational Progress. The authors of the study conclude that "for the past decade, nearly all reported test data show declines from grade 5 onwards. The declines become more pronounced at higher grade levels. This pattern is obvious in all tested areas."[1] Various commentators have attributed the declines to television viewing, to humanistic education, to a general movement away from the basics, to dropping enrollments in English courses, to changes in the length of the school day. A number of studies indicate that the most important factor in the test score decline may simply be *time on task*. If students do not enroll in English courses, their achievement scores drop.[2] If the length of the school day or year is cut, or if average daily attendance drops, then achievement scores also drop.[3]

Whatever the causes of the decline and whatever its meaning, various groups have used the fact of the decline as evidence that school programs are not what they should be. A pamphlet published by the Heritage Foundation, *Secular Humanism and the Schools,* begins with an exposition of the decline in SAT and ACT scores and goes on to argue that "secular humanism" has replaced the basics in the schools.[4] Whether or not that assertion is true is not so important as the fact that the decline has given critics tremendous leverage. Think how much less force would lie behind the assertion that secular humanism is rampant in the schools if there had been no drop in academic achievement.

The attacks launched against school programs seem, like Gaul, divisible into three parts: attacks against content, against methodology, and against ideology. Not only is the teaching of English open to attack in these areas, but in each area the English teacher is caught between almost diametrically opposed sides.

In the content area of grammar, for example, we have known since the publication of the Braddock study in 1963 that, and I quote, "In view of the widespread agreement of research studies based upon many types of students and teachers, the conclusion can be stated in strong and unqualified terms: the teaching of formal grammar has a negligible or, because it usually displaces some instruction and practice in actual composition, even a harmful effect on the improvement of writing."[5] On the other hand, many teachers of English have never abandoned grammar. And a pamphlet from the Council for Basic Education by Professor Kenneth Oliver argues that without formal grammar speakers of English will never get beyond a brand of local dialect that only "reflects and perpetuates local culture." Such language, the pamphlet continues, "represents a limited possibility for understanding, profiting by and contributing to the larger, total culture of America."[6] Oliver equates "understanding English" and using Standard English—as though a speaker of a local dialect is precluded from developing a large, effective vocabulary capable of dealing with complex and subtle ideas. He then attacks the rote learning of grammatical rules as tedious for students and as failing to "produce a sense of the relatedness of the materials learned." What is important, he argues, is learning "the principles of linguistic structure. . . . The teacher who does know and understand the basic principles can use any grammatical system that tells the truth about language."[7] And just what are these basic principles? The first is that "there are different word functions." Oliver then provides the familiar definitions of nouns and verbs. The basic principles of linguistic structure turn out to be the rules of traditional school grammar— right down to the diagramming of sentences. After making various grade level recommendations, he explains that "when the program briefly outlined here is adopted and carried through the tenth grade, many students will see the value of what they have done and of the potential for further learning that lies ahead."[8] Unfortunately, Professor Oliver never explains how learning these basic principles will enable children "to make the most of their native abilities" or "cope with the full range of human experiences." In fact, he does not even explain how learning these principles will help them write better compositions or get better scores on standardized tests.

Methodology has been a second prolific source of conflict. Parents have objected to laxity in classrooms, to allowing students too many choices, to grade inflation, to the abandonment of requirements. Although such objections, as far as I know, have never been consolidated into a major attack, they have contributed to a general public uneasiness about schooling. In part, such objections have contributed to the rapid rise of Christian schools across the country.

Some of the most extreme proponents of the unstructured classroom have recommended strongly against teacher planning. Robert Parker and Maxine Daly assert that "quite clearly, too much teacher planning ahead of time destroys the possibility of developing a truly student-centered, growth-promoting classroom." If one must plan, these writers recommend "only a certain amount of spadework . . . in the beginning."[9] Planning is only appropriate for teachers who feel uncomfortable in the ideal, unstructured classroom.

Ever since Neville Bennett's study on the relationship between teaching styles and pupil progress, however, recommendations for the unstructured, informal classroom have become increasingly suspect. Bennett found that achievement gains in reading, math, and English were higher in formal classes than in informal ones—with one exception. In one informal classroom, achievement gains were equal to or higher than those of the formal classrooms. In this classroom the teacher carefully structured and evaluated activities designed to effect cognitive outcomes. She also allowed children freedom of movement in the classroom. In short, although the learning environment was rather unstructured, the curriculum content was carefully structured.[10] An unstructured environment does not appear necessary to cognitive gains, but carefully structured curricular content does.

Many of the attacks on subject matter came as the result of very basic ideological conflicts. I refer particularly to the book protest that took place in Kanawha County, West Virginia, in 1974 and 1975. Various commentators have characterized these attacks as the revolt of those whose needs the schools have failed to meet, or of a "submerged social class." Many teachers and administrators believe them to be the result of a "monied" right wing conspiracy, the goal of which is to "take over public education."

While the protest involves elements of emotionalism, racism, class struggle, and even assistance from various conservative groups, evidence indicates that it derives its life from issues more basic than any of those interpretations suggests. The protest is rooted in a conflict between diametrically opposed beliefs about the nature of truth and human behavior. On the one side is found an unquestioning faith in revelation as the most important avenue to truth and guidance for human behavior; on the other, a belief in reason and empiricism that subjects all knowledge, including what is attained through revelation, to what Descartes called systematic doubt. The protesters see many signs of the latter, which they call "humanism," in textbooks. For them, the conflict between "creeping humanism" and their own values is of fundamental importance. Indeed, given the context of tax-supported schools and compulsory education, no resolution to the conflict may be possible without basic changes either in educational goals or in the principles governing our democracy.

The staunch, unflinching belief of the fundamentalists in the Bible as the revealed word of God and, therefore, as the most important source of truth has several ramifications. Two of these set fundamentalism apart from orthodox protestant churches: a belief in Biblical prophecy, especially prophecies pertaining to the return of Christ and

the millenium, and a belief in Satan as the powerful, highly intelligent enemy of man. When I interviewed various pastors in Kanawha
County and inquired about beliefs in the millenium, I was almost
invariably referred to a book called *The Late Great Planet Earth* by
Hal Lindsey and C.C. Carlson. Published in 1970, it is one of the most
popular books ever produced in the United States, having sold over
ten million copies in its first seven years. The book argues that since
1948 with the reestablishment of the state of Israel (one of the first
requirements for the fulfillment of the millenial prophecies), the "signs
of the times" indicate that Biblical prophecies are now in the process
of fulfillment. The Antichrist is abroad in the land, and the forces
are aligning themselves for the great confrontation. Satan, working
by indirection, is constantly among men and women—enrolling them
in his armies, luring them through secular philosophy and worldly
pleasure to abandon the teachings of Christ. In Kanawha County
when a splinter group composed of antibook people who had broken
with the official textbook review committee submitted its report to the
Board of Education, they prefaced the five hundred pages with a
quotation from a *McGuffey's Reader* of 1854:

> If you can induce a community to doubt the genuineness and
> authenticity of the Scriptures; to question the reality, and obliga-
> tions of religion; to hesitate in deciding whether there be any
> such thing as virtue or vice; whether there be an external state of
> retribution beyond the grave; or whether there exists any such
> being as God, you have broken down the barriers of moral virtue,
> and hoisted the flood gates of immorality and crime.

The fear of a humanism that chips away at Christian morality,
especially at a time when the millenium may be near, continues to
fuel protests against books and schools and to nourish the Christian
school movement. Clearly, if one result of education is to produce
individuals who question what they encounter, who do not accept the
old or the new at face value, who search for and create solutions to
problems, who do what is necessary for the creation of new knowledge, then education must be at loggerheads with the fundamentalists
and other groups who prefer to avoid such approaches to knowledge.

Christian fundamentalists are not the only ones who have voiced
disapproval of curricular content because of underlying ideology.
Even certain formerly sacrosanct literary works have become the focus
of conflict. Only a few years ago, for example, a small group of
parents whose children attended the New Trier (Illinois) high schools
wrote to the superintendent of schools:

> Our objection is to the use of *Huckleberry Finn* as required
> reading for classroom discussion in order to receive course
> credit. . . . Our primary objection is as follows:
>> The book is racially offensive and destructive to the self-image
>> and self-esteem of Black students who are required to partici-
>> pate in and endure classroom discussion of its contents. . . .
> Specifically, some of the points we see as self-evident are: Blacks
> in the book are commonly referred to as "niggers." The word
> "nigger" was derogatory during the period in which the book
> was written; today it is *outrageous* and *inflammatory*.

There is no need to dwell on the nature of these attacks, which are
undoubtedly all too familiar. The more important question is this:
Why do we seem to be so much more vulnerable to attack than
members of other professions? Other professions have their failure
rates, too. The legal system appears unable to reform even those felons
it is able to apprehend and convict—who, by the way, make up an
appallingly low percentage of those who commit felonies. Doctors
face an inevitable failure rate, which by the very nature of the human
condition is irreducible. Engineers have been unable to design air-
planes that do not crash, ships that do not sink, bridges that do not
collapse under stress. Chemists have not always produced synthetics
that do no harm to the environment. While such professionals have
been subject to attacks, the attacks have been directed at particular
flaws in a system that the public views as generally sound. A bridge
here and there may collapse into a river, but we do not distrust the
science of bridge building. Doctors necessarily lose more heart patients
than they save, but we are content to praise them for the lives they are
able to extend. Teaching, on the other hand, is subject to general
criticism, distrust, and perhaps even contempt. Although the exceptional case of a student saved may be praised, teaching as a whole is
often condemned as inefficient, or worse, as incompetent.

I see two major reasons for this wholesale condemnation. I'd like to
dispose of the first and go on to the second. Over three hundred years
of American education, people have assumed that just about anyone
can teach. Anyone who has knowledge can impart it to others. Everyone has been to school, so everyone knows what teachers do: they
present material, administer tests, take attendance, and give grades. It
is a familiarity that, unfortunately, breeds contempt. The second
reason for the general distrust of teaching at least contributes to that
contempt and is perhaps primarily responsible for it. This reason has
to do with what might be called the teacher's sense of professionalism.

Dan C. Lortie, in a sociological study of teaching entitled *Schoolteacher*, attempted to identify the ethos of teaching—"the pattern of

orientations and sentiments which is peculiar to teachers and which distinguishes them from the members of other occupations."[11] That discussion provides a number of insights.

The first is that teaching lacks the traditions of codified knowledge common to other professions. Let me quote:

> Special schooling for teachers is neither intellectually nor organi-
> zationally as complex as that found in the established professions.
> The study of medicine and engineering is rooted in science; law
> and divinity can point to generations of scholars who have con-
> tributed to their development. Neither holds for education, for
> specialized study of the subject has a short history and an erratic
> connection with the mainstream of intellectual development in
> modern society. Early study of education was isolated from schol-
> arship; attempts to integrate it with disciplines like psychology
> have lasted only a few decades. Nor do we find an equivalent to
> the centuries of codified experience encountered in law, engineer-
> ing, medicine, divinity, architecture, and accountancy; no way
> has been found to record and crystallize teaching for the benefit of
> beginners. Law students have their precedents, and engineers have
> exemplars dating back to ancient Rome; physicians recall Galen
> and centuries of empirical treatment, and clergymen can pore
> over thousands of published sermons and exegeses. Architects can
> examine monuments of success and failure, and the beginning
> student of accounting, although probably unknowingly, is work-
> ing with concepts dating back to medieval times and refined by
> generation upon generation of practical men. But what mean-
> ingful record exists of the millions of teaching transactions that
> have occurred since the City on the Hill?[12]

As English teachers we are only at the beginning of professionalizing our craft.

Lortie points out that much of the teacher's role is defined by the specifications of a curriculum. He goes on to say that while nearly all teachers want to add a personal touch, to allow themselves some leeway in the total curriculum, "there is little to suggest that class-room teachers struggle against the specifications included in such curricula." My own study of elective programs suggests that teach-ers do very little in the way of curricular planning or evaluation. The more than one hundred elective programs that I examined made few departures from traditional course work. In more than one school, the traditional tenth-, eleventh-, and twelfth-grade courses had simply been subdivided and sometimes expanded to provide mul-tiple offerings.[13]

Lortie's third point has to do with teacher pride in accomplish-ment. He points out that "the ideals of American public schools include two principles: the importance of equity in treatment and the assumption that all children can benefit from schooling." He discovers, however, that some teachers in his sample "cite effective work with all students as something 'extra,' as beyond the mere fulfillment of their duties."[14] Further, a large majority (64%) of teachers in the sample organize their discussions of pride in teaching around success with one student—the spectacular case. Nor did the teachers seem particularly worried about "the limited nature of success with one student."[15]

Lortie does not present these points as criticisms, nor do I. Indeed, historic and current social circumstances make such attitudes predictable. Teachers in general and English teachers in particular have had little training or encouragement to develop curricula at all—let alone in ways that will ensure coming closer and closer to the ideal of more efficient and more satisfying learning for increasingly greater percentages of students. But teachers in *every* school must begin the process of clarifying assumptions, establishing goals, and developing curricula, for English programs must withstand challenges school by school. Unless we begin moving toward that goal in logical and *demonstrable* steps, I fear our public will become increasingly disgruntled, administrators will presume to control curricula even more thoroughly than they do now, and we will attract into the profession more and more people who are merely time-servers.

The current back-to-basics movement is more than the beginning of such a trend. It moves control over curricular matters out of the hands of English and language arts teachers and puts it into the hands of lay people, administrators, and publishers. It specifies content as the learning of particular information and narrowly defined skills, but it leaves untouched the vast domain of learning to use language creatively and critically. It specifies a methodology that results in lockstep drill with teachers directing students through workbooks page by page, but it shuns the give-and-take among students and teachers that can, given appropriate focus, result in learning to use language precisely and effectively. And it implies an ideology of sorts—one which asserts that every question worth considering in schools has a right or wrong answer; therefore, it ignores the most important questions—the ones likely to convince students that language has value beyond the level of the most mundane activities.

Significant contributions to curricula require careful analysis of assumptions about what is important and why. Our answers to such questions are not likely to be definitive. The process of analysis will be a continuing one. But without it, our answers to questions of what and how to teach will be no more defensible than those of anyone else who enjoys conjecture. If we are to combat the triviality of such movements as back-to-basics, we must examine the fundamental questions of what we should teach and why. Each of the papers that follow provides a significant examination of these questions. Each, as it were, gets down to basics.

Notes

1. Annegret Harnischfeger and David E. Wiley, *Achievement Test Score Decline: Do We Need to Worry?* (St. Louis, Mo.: CEMREL, 1975), p. 69. Available from Central Midwestern Regional Educational Laboratory, 3120 Fifty-ninth Street, St. Louis, Missouri 63139–1799

2. Ibid.

3. Annegret Harnischfeger and David E. Wiley, "Schooling Cutbacks and Achievement Declines: Can We Afford Them?" *Administrator's Notebook*, 24, no. 1 (1975).

4. Onalee McGraw, *Secular Humanism in the Schools: The Issue Whose Time Has Come* (Washington, D.C.: Heritage Foundation, 1976).

5. Richard Braddock, Richard Lloyd-Jones, and Lowell Schoer, *Research in Written Composition* (Champaign, Ill.: National Council of Teachers of English, 1963), pp. 37–38.

6. Kenneth Oliver, *A Sound Curriculum in English Grammar: Guidelines for Teachers and Parents* (Washington, D.C.: Council for Basic Education, 1977), p. 1.

7. Oliver, p. 9.

8. Oliver, p. 42.

9. Robert P. Parker, Jr., and Maxine E. Daly, *Teaching English in the Secondary School* (New York: Free Press, 1973), pp. 73 and 78.

10. Neville Bennett with Joyce Jordan, George Long, and Barbara Wade, *Teaching Styles and Pupil Progress* (London: Open Books Publishing, 1976), pp. 79–102.

11. Dan C. Lortie, *Schoolteacher: A Sociological Study* (Chicago: University of Chicago Press, 1975), p. viii.

12. Lortie, pp. 58–59.

13. George Hillocks, Jr., *Alternatives in English: A Critical Appraisal of Elective Programs* (Urbana, Ill.: Educational Resources Information Center Clearinghouse on Reading and Communication Skills and National Council of Teachers of English, 1972).

14. Lortie, p. 115.

15. Lortie, p. 123.

Rhetoric, Mere Rhetoric, and Reality: Or, My Basics Are More Basic Than Your Basics

Wayne C. Booth
University of Chicago

Yesterday in Colorado Springs I saw a girl wearing a T-shirt that read, "70% unique." This morning I wonder whether I shouldn't be wearing one that says "2% original," or perhaps "1% useful," or "Significant at the .005 Level." Certainly I could proclaim myself "98% humble" as I think of the unlikelihood that anything I can say to you will be really helpful, either in the public relations task of addressing the new demands of the public or in that age-old, nobler task of trying to educate the young.

Like many would-be public advisers, I have less humility about suggesting what teachers should *not* do than I have about offering positive advice. One of my freshman students this year told me of a class he took last year as a senior in high school. His oral account was so lively that I asked him to write it up for me, and I'd like to read some of what he wrote.

> The year I entered high school the more liberal English teachers had decided to experiment with a new concept of education. Reading and writing would not be given the priority that they had in past years and would be overshadowed by the student's "development as a human being." The result of this change of heart was a number of new courses which we would be subject to. Among the courses offered was the seemingly harmless Themes in Literature. . . .
>
> The first day of class we were led into an unfurnished group meeting room which had no windows, full carpeting, and a garish color scheme. Our "lecturer" was a woman in her mid-fifties who sat down cross-legged in the circle we had formed, her heavy jewelry shattering the silence as she positioned herself, and began to describe what we would be doing for the next two months in her class. Themes in Literature was based on the belief that before we could gain any understanding of the "true beauty of literature" we must first understand ourselves and our relationship to others. She went on to describe how we could only learn to write by

freeing ourselves from our self-imposed restrictions and precon-
ceived notions of what writing should be. . . .

We were all very open-minded about the class, at first anyway,
and every one of us looked forward to our next meeting; after all,
we were the experimental generation. The next class eliminated
any doubts that I had about just how far the concept of experience
and encounter would be carried. When we arrived for class, we
found the floor covered with an assortment of pillows, bean-bag
chairs, and big foam cushions. We were told to make ourselves
comfortable, relax, and clear our minds. Then the lights went
out. Mrs. X stood in the corner with a poetry book titled something like *Reflections in an Empty Mirror,* reading with a pen-
light while the rest of us made a serious attempt to release our
inner beings. I really enjoyed it at first. It was certainly more
enjoyable than arguing about our papers or taking notes, but
after about twenty minutes of listening to that nonsense about
how we should leave our bodies behind in space and let our
spirits merge into the ever-flowing abyss, I wanted either to go to
sleep or to tell the teacher to shut up. Finally our tranquility was
abruptly interrupted by the inevitable joker who takes advantage
of every opportunity to get his hands into a girl's pants. First the
girl started giggling, then out came something like, "Oh, Paul,
stop it!" Well, by this time even the people who were asleep woke
up and the class erupted in laughter. Mrs. X quickly turned on
the lights; she was noticeably embarrassed.

Well, now that we had "transcended" our senses, it was time
for direct sensory contact. Mrs. X randomly selected partners from
around the room and ordered them to touch each other in the
most unlikely places (i.e., knee caps, Adam's apples, ear lobes)
and then describe out loud to the class what they were feeling. It
was insane. . . .

Well, to make a long story short, our one writing assignment
consisted of being led into a room full of incredibly corny posters,
obviously ordered from *Senior Scholastic* (i.e., the high school
version of the *Weekly Reader*), then choosing one which emotionally moved us and writing about it. Our final most important
project was an *art* assignment which we were to display to the
class along with an oral presentation about how the project
symbolized our inner being. . . . I was not bitter about the class,
after all, we were the experimental generation. When our older
brothers and sisters were burning down college campuses while
we were in grade school, it was decided that something was wrong
with our educational system. We were going to be different. I had
come to accept things like this as part of the game and, believe
me, this was not the worst.

When I heard about that classroom, I wanted to shout, as so many
are doing these days, "Back to the basics!" While John was lying on
the floor laughing at his teacher, he obviously was not learning any
of the skills that would have helped him be a better student in my

freshman humanities course. The world's literature and philosophy and history lay untouched as he lay there being touched. Whole domains of grammar and syntax were left as mysteries as he explored the mystery of his being. And the essential art of making one sentence follow another was unmentioned as he created a so-called work of art that he held in contempt.

Perhaps most of us want to get back to the basics, in one sense or another, but I don't have to tell you that we are not exactly united in a single conception of what the basics might be. We just fall into whatever comes to mind as "obviously essential," without taking a lot of time to think hard about it. Wayland Young once began his serious history and sociological analysis of prostitution, called *Sitting on a Fortune,* with the guess that nobody in the history of the race had ever spent so much as four hours *thinking* about that ancient institution. Well, I'm sure that many people have spent at least four hours trying to think about education, but you wouldn't think so, to judge from the careless diagnoses and simplistic prescriptions that fill the air.

My anecdote about John itself requires some thought because it seems to suggest the perhaps self-serving assumption that what John really needed in high school was simply preparation for my college course, where the basics are reading fairly difficult classics and learning to write and talk about them: *The Odyssey,* Thucydides' *History,* Shakespeare, Freud's *Civilization and Its Discontents,* Karl Marx.

Karl Marx! Can you hear the great public scream? Karl Marx a basic? Meanwhile others fall, with the same sense of naturalness, into conceptions that seem to us more absurd. I was amused when the associate director of the Council for Basic Education, George Weber, talking about how widespread is the back-to-basics move and how much progress was being made, offered this observation as a major piece of evidence: "People are talking about spelling for the first time in several decades. Grammar is coming back to the schools. It's no longer a dirty word." Well, spelling and grammar are not dirty words in my vocabulary either, but, like you, I know from experience what happens to an English classroom when such basics are made the center of instruction. What happens is that we produce graduates who say they hate English, who think of English teachers as pedants or torturers or both, and who do their best whenever in later life they actually meet one of us creatures who say we "teach English" to escape to more friendly territory.

So we have big differences, at least on the surface, between ourselves and our various publics. And these differences are represented within the profession, not just "out there." But I'd like to argue that beneath the differences we can discover common ground, that indeed the most important single task for this decade is to find ways of talking about our common ground so that we may educate ourselves and our various publics to its importance. Our task is thus both to discover whatever is really basic to education and to find ways of talking about it that will show why what *we care about doing* is what the *public really wants done.*

In other words, I think we are doomed to fail if we see our task as merely improving public relations or, as it is often put, "reestablishing our credibility with the public." We do want the public to believe in us, but if we are to find the language needed to talk to the public, we must first find the language to describe to each other our own commitment. And that will take more hard thought than most of our suggested cures seem to be based on.

I wish I had a respectable sample of the kind of talk that might persuade the public to trust us as we decide what to do next. Instead, I must address that preliminary half of our task, the effort to become clear with each other about *why we do what we do.* It could be argued that much of the public's distrust of what we have been doing springs from our own anxiety about whether what we do is really important. Because we have lacked collective confidence in teaching our students how to read and think and write, we have let our subject be represented by every new fad under the sun. For all the public can tell from our statements, we teachers think that any old subject is as good as any other old subject, that learning how to read and write well has no priority over hundreds of other lively and novel subjects. We seem to demand that they pay us just as happily for practicing amateur Zen Buddhism or T-group formations or whatever elective occurs to us as useful for developing literate citizens. When the public sees us unsure of why English should be the center of the curriculum, when the public sees us unwilling to defend what we do as essential both to our society and to every member of our society, they naturally feel some confidence in saying, "OK, *you've* given up on the job. Let *us* tell you what to do. Now what you should do is make a list of elementary standards for literacy, and then you should teach each standard, drill by drill, and then you should make up competency examinations to test each standard, and then we'll be sure that everybody you graduate is literate."

I am a bit troubled by the seeming suggestion—perhaps I misunderstand—that we should go about answering such demands by fitting into our classes short bursts of teaching that we ourselves do not respect: as if to say, "We'll spend the month or so necessary to pass the competency exams and save the rest of our time for genuine education." Good advice, perhaps, for short-term survival. But when we do that we are simply educating the public to believe in their own misguided notions—if they *are* misguided—and to believe in our hypocrisy, when they find us out. What is worse, our contempt for the competencies we sneak in this way will be all too apparent to our students, our critical audience.

I would suggest instead that we go about it the other way 'round, that if we think hard enough about our own notions of the basics, and then teach with full devotion according to those notions, we will find the competencies following quite naturally. Brave words, perhaps, but I am deeply convinced that any teacher who is fully engaged in learning to read and think and write—a lifelong task for us all—and who discovers how to engage students in wanting to read and think and write, any teacher who is mentally *engaged* with life, will find the competencies the public really wants following quite naturally.

A loose phrase like "learning to read and think and write" covers a lot of territory, and I can touch here on only one central plot in that territory, what some have called the survival skills, the skills demanded of everyone who must cope with American life in our time. In other words, I'm not thinking mainly of learning how to read Shakespeare or Homer and of how to write passable critical essays on them; one can *survive* in modern America without being able to do that. Rather, I am thinking of the simple matter of learning to understand what people are really saying, learning to look at what words really mean, and learning to respond with words that do important work in the world. Sometimes we call such basics the language arts, sometimes communication skills, and sometimes even harsher terms than that. I choose to call this subject rhetoric, though I know that to do so will already seem to have given the show away. I can hear someone say, "If you try to convince the public that what we are experts in is rhetoric, that what we are making of our charges is excellent rhetoricians, that public will *know* that they must now take over; we've lost our marbles." Well, maybe so. I surely don't want to quarrel over a name, and if you have a better name for the subject, the whole art of improving our capacity to interpret what other people say, to think about it, and then to say something worthwhile in return, then use that word.

It is certainly true that the word *rhetoric* has a bad press these days. As I was preparing these remarks, I read in *The New Yorker* the following statement:

La lutte pour la France is over for a while—with casualties to the
language which could keep a whole generation of academicians
off the dole. It was a battle of words, and it went on for so long
that by the time the French actually got to the polls to vote this
spring, those words out of the litanies of left and right had lost
any reference to reality they might have had and turned completely senseless and rhetorical.[1]

Similarly, in a recent *Wall Street Journal* I read a column headed
"Rhetoric vs. Reality." The discussion was about the statistics of
inflation, on the one hand, which is of course "reality," and what
people are saying to describe inflation and to cure it on the other
hand—obviously something that is *not* reality, namely rhetoric.

But we shouldn't make the mistake of thinking that it is only the
word rhetoric that has a bad press. It is our whole subject—the entire
range of language and its resources—that is often meant when people
contrast hard reality with the stuff you and I try to teach. Writing
about her first book, Betty Friedan noted recently that her rhetoric
was not "meant to take the place of action." "Wasn't it Marx," she
asks, "who said, 'You can't fight a revolution and write a book at the
same time'?" And a final example: the Suffragettes had a slogan,
"Deeds Not Words"—as clear a statement as we could want that words
are not deeds.

There are so many implacable moments in life, moments that can't
be changed very much by words, that this way of distinguishing
something over here as "reality" and *something over there* as "rhetoric"—mere style or language—comes to seem justified. After all, most
of us believe that rhetoric, even when addressed to God himself, can't
make a good crop grow unless the farmer has first done the plowing
and planting. When the earthquake comes, rhetoric about architecture
can't change the hard facts that some buildings are well built and
don't fall down and some other buildings are badly built and do fall
down. No wonder that most of us, even the professors of rhetoric,
have developed metaphors for two domains that imply a sharp
distinction: words *approach* reality, we say, words *grapple* with
reality, reach for it; they are a *tool* for dealing with reality, or a
lattice or *screen* to obscure it. Without simplifying too much, we
could say that most scientific achievements of the last three hundred
years have been based on such a distinction, leading to the effort
to see behind or through our misleading words to the hard stuff:
reality. You have only to look at the harsh words about rhetoric
written by philosophers like Locke to see how deep this sharp distinction runs in modern thought.

Two years ago one of Adolph Hitler's right-hand men, Albert Speer, published his memoirs and tried among other things to understand how Hitler had been able to "take him in." Speer finally attributed Hitler's otherwise incredible power over those around him to Hitler's knowledge of human psychology and his genius in using words to play upon the weakness of others. Commenting on Speer's confessions, a writer in *Encounter* observes that Hitler's primary skill was in oratory. His oratory "was of the kind that speaks neither to the mind nor to the heart of his audience, but plays upon its nerves until they are strung to such a pitch of intensity that they shriek for release in action. . . . But it can only be practised by one who has a profound and subtle understanding of the secret hopes and fears of his audience . . . , who can be a conservative with the conservative, a revolutionary with the revolutionary, a man of peace with the pacifist and a war lord with the belligerent, and on occasions all these things at once should it be necessary. Certainly Hitler was the greatest master of this type of oratory there has ever been, and I have stood among 10,000 people in the *Sportpalast* in Berlin and known that everyone around me was the victim of its spell. Who knows, if I had not been inoculated in childhood against the tricks of oratory, I might have succumbed myself." [2]

Notice that word *inoculated*. Rhetoric is in this view something to be inoculated against—and who wouldn't want to be inoculated against rhetoric like Hitler's?

Suppose we begin by accepting this negative notion of rhetoric as trickery or cover-up or obfuscation, the opposite of reality or genuine action. It would seem obvious that if we are surrounded by such stuff, dangerous as can be, one major task for students and teachers, regardless of what their specialty is called, is precisely to get inoculated against the dangerous disease. "We're surrounded by pollution, they're out there, ready to destroy us! Man the test tubes, mount the microscopes, start up the computers, so that we can exercise the manly art of self-defense, using reality against rhetoric." If anything is basic, surely such an art must be.

We really do seem to be surrounded by masters of rhetoric, many of them professional liars using rhetoric to trap us. Every day millions of Americans are taken in by public words that no educated person would believe without careful thought and investigation. The public has thus a vast interest, whether it knows it or not, in any education that attends to words and their ways. I'm not thinking simply of the many hoaxes, the fake biographies of Howard Hughes, the equally fake but subtler fictions by Castaneda about his marvelous Indian guru. I am thinking of the flood of falsehood and half-truth that spews from our presses and television sets daily.

To a great deal of what is daily *uttered at them,* our students should learn to say an unqualified no. In judging advertising I can often say an outright no, without waiting for conclusive proof, because the motives for lying are so obvious. "Come to where the flavor is, come to Marlboro country." No, thanks, I'll stay right here, thanks anyway for the sincere invitation. "BP Oil is a new, 100% British company. As a new company we have a new slogan: Working harder for everyone. It's not advertising puffery. We actually mean it." No, no you don't! I can say no with great confidence. You *don't* actually mean it. You mean, "Buy BP oil!" "Asia provides the wonder, we make it wonderful!—Holiday Inn, the most accommodating people in the world." No, no, no!

Learning when to say no to words in the name of reality is thus surely one of the most liberal—that is, liberating, of all the arts. It can often simply be the *no* of laughter, the laughter of ridicule. Perhaps you have seen a recent collection of metaphorical boo-boos made by members of Congress. The collector, a Washington journalist, called his little gems malaphors: not metaphors, not malapropisms, but malaphors. He has been listening to the way our representatives talk, and he hears them say things like this: "He threw a cold shoulder on that idea." Or, "Now we've got to flush out the skeleton." Or, "He deals out of both ends of his mouth." One thing that most of us do almost automatically is teach our students to put up their dukes against such stuff—and in doing so we are really doing part of what the public wants us to do—or would, if they knew their true interests.

Now I don't think what I have been saying so far is false in any obvious way, but I hope that by now you are impatient with a certain emptiness in what I have offered, its negativeness, its defensiveness, its limited applicability. If your whole duty is to learn how to reject false words and thus get at a hard reality distinct from those words, how do you recognize *true* words when you see them? What should I do, for example, if I am a believer in Hitler and I hear a piece of very powerful oratory *attacking* his aims and methods. Should I congratulate myself on having been inoculated in my childhood against oratory? Obviously, a simple self-defensive suspicion will be of no help whatever to me there. The real problem will be to recognize that *now is the time to believe* the orator and give up my old beliefs.

But the trouble goes even further than that. It is not just that we need to study how to discover when rhetoric should be accepted because it *really reflects* reality; we need to study and teach a totally different view of what rhetoric is and what reality is.

In its simplest terms the error so far can be described as forgetting that rhetoric does not always either *reflect* reality, at best, or *distort* it, at worst; rather, rhetoric often *makes* reality. The words and other symbols we use together often *are* reality, the truth, the world with which we must deal. And they often become a reality just as hard, in the sense of producing changes in other realities, as the most resistant stone or star.

Sometimes rhetoric makes a reality, *becomes* a reality, *is* a reality that is not just something suitable to the maker, not just a private illusion, but a reality that is real precisely in that basic sense we mean when we say that this room and those chairs and the flesh of your hand are real—a reality that has to be acknowledged by every honest observer. It dictates, in other words, what everybody else *ought* to say about it. We may not want to label it "objective" because in one sense we always have only our "subjective" pictures, and they can be encountered and tested only in our experience. But it is not simply subjective either, in the sense of depending on this or that person's private view. Perhaps for now we can be satisfied simply by calling it *real*. We might then use some word like *intersubjective* for our agreements about it.

In talking of ways in which rhetoric makes reality, I'd like to use a classification that theorists have used ever since Aristotle. Some words, called deliberative rhetoric, are directed to making the future; some words judge the past (forensic rhetoric); and some words (epideictic rhetoric) change our views about, and thus remake, the present. Starting with that limp but useful triad, I'll work toward a point that I think Aristotle and many others have understated: when words make your past, present, and future, what they really make is *you*, and thus all of them have what might be called an epideictic center.

We start with the future, where my case is the most obvious. Once you think about how our words *make* the future, it is surprising that anybody could ever have thought that the language we teach only *reflects* reality. Everybody assumes, in practice, that debate about what to do next somehow changes what we actually *do* next, so that the future is made, at least to some degree, in how I talk about it right now. Families argue about where to take their vacation, and the reality of the vacation is changed by the argument. (Of course there are in such moments also changes in the reality of the present. If the argument is a pleasant one, the present is made more fun; if it is an unpleasant one, the present is less fun. In either case they are making some present reality *of that kind.*)

Such *deliberative* rhetoric, as it was traditionally called, can produce results as hard as bullets, since it often literally determines who will die and who will live. In a way everybody knows this. It is denied only when people talk theoretically about whether human beings have free choice, or when theorists of language just plain forget what language in fact does. When people say "Cut the cackle and get down to the hard facts," they exhibit in that statement itself a wish that the statement will change the future—that it will at least "cut the cackle."

You will remember my quotation from Betty Friedan, saying that her *words* were never meant "to take the place of *action* that might change society." What do you suppose she turned to when she stopped "depending on words," as she put it? "Why," she said, "I threw myself into the action"—and the list of actions turns out to be: "I lectured, drafted statements of purpose, interviewed, kept a public diary, and wrote reports and articles." That's all the *action* she lists. That's "getting away from the words and getting down to the action." I don't think she was silly to say that, though we all find it amusing. I think her comment illustrates that we are talking about two kinds, or phases, of real action, not a distinction between rhetoric and reality.

Important as our deliberative rhetoric is in determining future realities, I am more interested here in the curious way in which its effects spill backwards, as it were, into the present. It was always clear that epideictic rhetoric could make the difference between good life and bad. When we praise or blame each other, lament our losses, celebrate our victories, eulogize our heroes and institutions, we can make or break a given day or year or epoch. How we talk about it changes what it is. But there is an interesting sense in which our deliberative or political rhetoric effects the same kind of transformation of reality. Since it is a process hardly ever talked about, and since the great public that cares about basics has an immense stake in it, I shall spend the rest of this paper trying to make that point clear.

Since there is some danger that some of you might consider my thinking a bit mushy from here on, I'm going to offer one of those queer things that every talk on rhetoric ought to have at least one of—a good solid *sorites.* Aristotle, you remember, says that a sorites— that is, a chain of syllogisms—should never be too long or too short. Sound advice, and I have of course followed it. The first syllogism:

> *Major premise:* Individual freedom is a fundamental value we all pursue, and indeed ought to pursue, as essential to all else

that we value. We could discuss this premise but I assume that we don't need to here.

Minor premise: Individual freedom depends on political institutions that operate through politics—that is, through a political process of give-and-take, of talking things out, of seeking reasonable compromise—rather than through the imposition of force or the will of one leader or group. I must say something in a moment about this minor premise because it is not self-evident, but first, the conclusion to this first syllogism.

Therefore: Politics is a major value that we all pursue and indeed ought to pursue. Instead of being a naughty word, politics is, or are, the only defense we have against the tyranny either of a single tyrant or of whatever group at a given moment has the power to impose its collective will.

We should pause for a moment in our pursuit of rigorous logic to discuss the minor premise that landed us in the embarrassing spot of saying a good word for politics. We could in fact spend considerable time on the reasons for saying that our individual freedom depends on politics. What I will do instead is recommend to you a marvelous little book by Bernard Crick, *In Defence of Politics.* His brief and witty argument boils down to this: when interests of various groups and judgments by members of those groups clash, as they always will in any fully human society, how many ways are there to resolve the differences? There are in fact only two: either a single position or answer can be imposed by force or the threat of force, or the contending interests can seek a political solution—that is, a solution that depends on accommodation among interests. Crick puts it this way:

> Common usage of the word might encourage one to think that politics is a real force in every organised state. But a moment's reflection should reveal that this common usage can be highly misleading. For politics, as Aristotle points out, is only one possible solution to the problem of order. It is by no means the most usual. Tyranny is the most obvious alternative—the rule of one strong man in his own interest; and oligarchy is the next most obvious alternative—the rule of one group in their own interest. The method of rule of the tyrant and the oligarch is quite simply to clobber, coerce or overawe all or most of these other groups in the interest of their own. The political method of rule is to listen to these other groups so as to conciliate them as far as possible, and to give them a legal position, a sense of security, some clear and reasonably safe means of articulation, by which these other groups can and will speak freely. Ideally politics draws all these

groups into each other so that they each and together can make a
positive contribution towards the general business of government,
the maintaining of order. . . . But, however imperfectly this process of deliberate conciliation works, it is nevertheless radically
different from tyranny, oligarchy, kingship, dictatorship, despot-
ism and—what is probably the only distinctively modern type of
rule—totalitarianism.[3]

Crick has now prepared us for the second syllogism. As in all
sorites, our new major premise is the conclusion of the previous
syllogism:

> *Major premise:* Politics is immensely important to all of us, our
> only defense against tyranny.
>
> *Minor premise:* The quality and success of any truly political
> process will depend on the quality of the rhetorical exchange
> among the participants—that is, you and me. We can here pick
> up from Crick's statement the phrases "listen to these other
> groups" and "means of articulation." Again this will take some
> discussion, but you can see ahead to the next statement.
>
> *Therefore:* Improving our rhetoric is our best defense, our only
> alternative to tyranny.

(Perhaps we should note that the threat of force in itself can be
considered a form of rhetoric, but it is surely a degraded form, "mere"
rhetoric often hard to distinguish from the use of force itself; it is in
fact force disguised as words, words that indeed obscure reality.)

Again in this second syllogism, it is the minor premise that raises
the questions. What can it mean to say that the quality of any political
process depends on the quality of the rhetoric available to the politicians? Most of us have some general sense that this is true, but it is
not an easy proposition to prove to anyone who is determined to
doubt it.

Yet it is surely true. Perhaps it is most obviously seen to be true in
the matter of public lying. A society that encourages lying and depends on it for its functioning obviously cannot long endure without
tyranny. The exchange of reasons among contending interests depends
on maintaining some level of integrity and hence trust so that reasons
can be in reality exchanged. It seems obvious that if any society ever
reaches a point at which everyone can always assume that in all
likelihood everyone else is lying, the political process in our sense is
dead, and the resulting inhuman chaos will soon be resolved by some
tyrannical takeover. Thus what we call political corruption is a *real*
corruption, a corruption of rhetoric. If it goes beyond a certain point,

always hard to determine, we are doomed. One often wonders how close we are to that point in America. I doubt that public lying has ever been as profitable as it is today.

One thinks inevitably in this connection of recent books by Haldeman and Nixon, immensely profitable mixtures of lies, half-truths, and perhaps even truth, though there is no reason to expect it. I loved Sam Erwin's recent statement about Haldeman's book: "I would believe what Haldeman says only if it was testified to by all the apostles except Judas. It's not entirely unlikely that a man who has lied when under oath might conceivably lie when not under oath." But the trouble is that our lives are filled with too many Haldemans and Nixons for the Sam Erwins to keep up with them. And the point is that they are bad not just for our deliberative rhetoric: they pollute our political atmosphere, they degrade our lives—right now in the present.

Perhaps that is enough as hint about the minor premise of syllogism number two. Let me hurry on to my third syllogism; again the major premise is the conclusion of the previous syllogism:

> *Major premise:* Improving our rhetoric is our only alternative to tyranny.

> *Minor premise:* Our best hope for improving our rhetoric is improvement in rhetorical education.

> *Conclusion:* Well, I'm almost embarrassed to say it, it seems just a bit self-serving to announce that you and I are charged by our society to teach each other how to read and write, listen, think, and speak; that we are charged, in other words, with improving the arts of rhetoric; that we are society's front-line troops not only against tyranny in the future but against the dehumanizing of our lives right now. Embarrassing as any particular phrase of self-anointing may sound to our own ears, the fact remains: Everything we value in our society depends, directly or indirectly, on our ability to teach each other about how to think about what people say—not only the defensive rhetoric of smoking out the liars and thieves, but the affirmative art of sorting out the maybes, discovering our true friends and true interests, and marshalling the forces of language on behalf of our true interests as we find them. Self-centered or not, I see no escape from the conclusion that liberal education as the study of rhetoric is our best hope for preserving the possibility of free activity of any kind, including all other kinds of study and every hope the public has of influencing the schools—every hope except the illusory one—the big boss on a white horse.

That might be a good place to end, but the discovery of our responsibility is obviously only a beginning. Where do we move, when the syllogisms have done what they can do?

I think the first point should be a warning about where *not* to move. Our potential as a political force can avoid corruption only to the degree that it is not turned into a particular political faction. If we teachers try to organize our students, or talk them into lining up behind any one specific program that we happen to like, instead of teaching them the arts of rhetorical analysis and exchange, our peda-gogical rhetoric will immediately turn into *mere* rhetoric, regardless of the virtues in our cause. Having taught them merely a line of action we think good because it may build some kind of desirable future, we will have neglected to teach them how to deal thoughtfully and effectively on behalf of causes that you and I have not yet dreamed of.

The second point follows. Much of what we must do will not look like politics, and it will often be called something other than rhetoric. Though I have talked mainly of political rhetoric, as an example of how reality is made by rhetoric, I hope you can see how the same point applies to every nook and cranny of our lives. We not only affect future reality as we debate what we should do; we also affect the reality of our lives right now. We change ourselves with every kind of rhetorical exchange; and the changes then produce further effects. The reality that is most decisively made in every kind of rhetoric our students meet is people, the very shapes of their minds and souls. When historians, for example, make and remake our past, what are they really making? They are making new versions of you and me. I am in large part what I think my past was. If I have no roots, I am vulnerable. Give me good roots and I can flourish. Again, when the pseudoanthropologists tell us that we are essentially naked apes or creatures with a territorial imperative or weapon wielders, they are making and remaking our very natures, so malleable are we all. And when novelists, playwrights, and poets tell us and our students that we are lost miserable creatures caught in a life that is a swindle, a slaughterhouse, a madhouse, a rat race, a con game, a carnal house, a whorehouse, the lowest circle of hell, a raging inferno, a pigsty—to use only a few of the current metaphors they offer—they change not just our picture of what *other* people are, they change what *we* are, both as we read and as we move after reading. Such metaphors are not just the sea we swim in (though that is a much better notion than saying that they are "the screen through which we observe" or "our tools for grappling with reality"); they are the air we breathe, or even better, our psychic food. We are what we have eaten. Our minds and souls have been made mainly out of other people's rhetoric.

It takes no very deep analysis of the current scene to conclude that we consume a daily diet that is nine-tenths poison. Half of the other tenth is pablum, baby food designed deliberately to keep us from ever growing up. To run through the list of the dyshumanities that the great American society forces on us daily would take too long—just think of the images of humankind, of our possibilities, that are projected by what Tom Wolfe calls the one-hand magazines, by the novels we are most likely to pick up from the drugstore rack, by television ads and standard television dramas, by the typical political appeal. But once I get warmed up, I'll become more preachy than I've already been. I must resist that, and conclude instead with some suggestion about how my claims about rhetoric could be generalized to the other aspects of our lives as teachers.

What I have tried to do is to suggest why what the public really wants is also what we want. We *are* the public, in the matter of consuming and responding to a flood of rhetoric that on the one hand seems nine-tenths lies but on the other is the very lifeblood of our democratic survival. It is inconceivable to me that any teacher who takes education seriously in these terms would not get personally engaged in reading and thinking and writing, or that students educated by such a teacher would not master the elementary competencies. When and where to deal directly with comma splices cannot be decided in a general way, though each school should surely make clear decisions about which grades are to be responsible for which minimal skills. My point is that when teachers and students are fully engaged with the world's rhetoric, including their own, competence in handling the elements will follow as naturally as the performance knowledge of grammar follows the child's desire to learn to talk. Students who care about their rhetorical effect will soon learn that they can betray themselves with bad punctuation and spelling, but they will also learn that what is bad punctuation and spelling and grammar in one rhetorical climate may perhaps be good in another, and that the details of what any rhetor does will always be determined by the desire to establish a bond with some other human being.

I must underline in conclusion two points that may already be obvious. The first is that the education in rhetoric that I am talking about will for the most part be conducted under some other name, and that it cannot be achieved by English teachers working without the help of colleagues in other subjects. It may be pursued under names like language arts or civics or popular culture or history or general science or film criticism or simply reading and writing. It may indeed be taught by teachers who have never heard the word *rhetoric* except as a term of abuse.

The second point is that what I have said about rhetoric is only a sample of what we might want to say about other values we care for. You may have noted that in defending rhetoric I seemed to have scuttled Shakespeare and Homer because, as I said, students can in some sense survive without Shakespeare and Homer as they cannot survive without mastering the arts of rhetoric. Clearly, I do not intend to scuttle the study of the world's great literature. I am convinced that we share with the public—in spite of the fact that many members of the public do not know it—as deep a common interest in *literary* education as we have in rhetorical education. But to make that common interest clear will require of us much thought and many different efforts at translation of the kind I have attempted here concerning this other common interest. And the same can be said of any other deep value that the public seems to ignore when it calls for spelling bees: knowledge of history, of the physical sciences, of mathematics beyond arithmetical skills. What this means is that in electing to be educators we have elected to be educators of the adult public as well as of our charges. But it also means that we have elected to make a life-time project of educating ourselves. Nothing of what we would defend can be defended by people who do not care for it enough to practice it as a daily habit. If we do not read and think and speak and write with a loving attention to how words can create or destroy, we'll never convince the public that their view of things is stunted and self-destructive.

To work at improving one's own education is hard; to try to teach other people how to improve theirs is much harder. But to attempt to improve a nation's educational climate seems at times an almost hopeless task. We do, however, have many resources on our side, you and I, including our vast inheritance of great novels, plays, poems, speeches, constitutions, philosophical works, histories, and theories of rhetoric and literary criticism of the past and present. We also have, or so I like to think, a natural hunger for something better than we are fed on all sides. I may be wrong about that natural hunger. It may be, for all anyone can prove, that any culture whose children spend four to eight hours a day with television and then spend their remaining hours in school with harried teachers who must teach from eviscerated textbooks designed by programmers trying to drill one micro-concept at a time—it *may* be that such a culture will be permanently crippled, molded in shapes of desire and fulfillment that make real growth impossible. I refuse to believe it, but the experience of every teacher—from the first grade on—shows that even if education is our best hope, it is a slim one.

I would like to end on a more cheerful note, but I cannot. I do not *know* that we are not now on a hopelessly irreversible downward spiral. What I do claim, however, is that the issues at stake in our conflicts about the "basics" are the most important reality we know: what the life of humankind now is and what it will be.

Notes

1. Jane Kramer, "A Reporter in Europe (France)," *The New Yorker,* 19 June 1978, p. 71.

2. *Encounter,* November 1975, p. 44.

3. Bernard Crick, *In Defence of Politics,* 2d ed. (Chicago and London: University of Chicago Press, 1972), pp. 18–19.

The Collision of the Basics Movement with Current Research in Writing and Language

James R. Squire
Senior Vice-President, Ginn and Company

According to the most recent information, some thirty-four states have established programs to assess pupil competencies in basic skills contrasted with only a handful sixteen months ago. Such is the strength of the back-to-basics movement that the number of states committed to competency testing seems likely to swell to a good four dozen by the end of the year; that number at least is presently considering some kind of an examination program. The fact is that our citizens themselves—through school board members, legislators, elected officials, and more outspoken opinion leaders—are forcing new attention to basic standards, despite the worries and admonitions of educators over the impact of competency testing in the schools.[1] Approaches are far from uniform but the intent remains the same whether children are tested at grades three, six, eight, and eleven, tested prior to the awarding of a secondary school diploma, or tested at least once in every grade. All seek to redirect educational priorities through systematic assessment of minimal competence in basic skills.

It is instructive, I think, to note that virtually all competency programs deal with pupil performance in reading and in computational skills; more than half concern themselves either with writing or with the language skills that parents associate with writing. Only rarely do we find states and districts testing in the sciences or social sciences. In every curricular area, "life skills" or "coping skills" or "survival skills" are stressed; i.e., those applications of basic skills that pertain to success in meeting day-to-day challenges (placing emergency telephone calls, reading labels on household poisons, writing brief messages and reports) rather than to mastery of academic applications such as the study skills needed in school and college. Insofar as life skills are concerned, we have assumed transfer, which has not always occurred.

But the national concern over the quality of student writing extends far beyond the emphasis on competency testing, which focuses really only on the least able of our pupils. The decline in SAT scores that began during the mid-sixties has so mesmerized parents, media, and psychometricians that it has required more than three years of intensive effort to explain why today's children perform less adequately than their aunts and uncles of a decade ago.[2] Indeed, not until the National Association of Secondary School Principals released its recommendations this past spring have many responsible leaders been willing to admit directly what parents have long suspected—that the reduced levels of challenge and lower standards in today's programs of instruction may be a basic cause of the deterioration in pupil writing.[3] Reports documenting disturbing conditions continue to appear. We have the Koerner report on the state of writing to the Sloan Foundation; the Graves report to the Ford Foundation; and the varied reports from the National Assessment of Educational Progress, which show a decline in pupil performance in writing after grade four, but a decline that focuses less on children's competence in spelling and mechanics than on their inability to handle transitions, to control complex sentence structures, and to edit papers that have already been written.[4] These reports—together with informal observations by supervisors and administrators—raise serious questions about the quality and the amount of instruction and practice that children are receiving in writing, a concern well documented in Arthur Applebee's report on high school teaching conditions.[5] Applebee finds, some fifteen years after the National High School Study of English Programs, schools still expending time and effort in much the same way. Sixty-six percent of instructional time remains devoted to literature, largely to *belles lettres,* a kind of reading unlikely to provide much support for the expository writing required elsewhere in high school programs.

There are reasons then for the extensive concern with the teaching of writing, reasons why conferences and conventions find sessions on teaching writing swamped by interested participants, reasons for the virtual nationalization of the Bay Area Writing Project, reasons why exhibitors at professional meetings report customers quickly exhausting available supplies of workbooks that focus on aspects of writing, reasons for the return of the "golden oldies" among the textbooks most widely used in this country, reasons to suspect that many of today's developments are on collision course with research in the teaching of writing and language development. Not since the early sixties and the halcyon days of the National Defense Education Act and the Commission on English of the College Entrance Examination Board has the teaching of writing so gripped professional attention. But perhaps, as Leo Munday recently tried to demonstrate in a study of standardized test scores over the years, the early sixties may well have represented the high watermark of pupil attainment in the history of public education.[6]

Out of this present melange of advice and admonition, collision and clarification, emerge four touchstones that may help schools find their way in reconciling today's requirements with what we now know from research about the processes of writing and composing: (1) time on instructional task is critical in improving learning; (2) instruction must deal with a variety of language functions and provide time on task for each; (3) instruction must distinguish between the processes of composing and basic supportive skills; (4) consideration of the complete process of composing helps to identify the most teachable moments for providing instruction in the various dimensions of composing.

Improving Learning through Time on Task

To improve the reading performance of primary school children during recent years, most schools doubled the time spent on instructional tasks in reading. As time on key reading tasks increased, pupil performance on tests improved. Clearly we have demonstrated the success of this phenomenon. Similarly, then, to improve the competence of children in writing, we must provide more opportunities for them to write. Writing alone may not be sufficient to produce good and effective writers, but without extensive experience in writing, children are not likely to make significant progress.

The increase over the past decade in sales to schools of plain copying paper and the precipitous decrease in sales of lined handwriting paper reflect the decline in the amount of writing required in our classrooms and the increased use of duplicated drill sheets. From the first grade on, boys and girls are capable of completing two or three pieces of independent writing a week, yet how few of them are given the opportunity.[7] No one really knows how often children and young people do write today, but informal studies and conversations with supervisors suggest that rarely are the majority of children asked to write more than three or four times in a semester.

The time-on-task phenomenon also suggests that we can produce substantial improvement in pupil performance on many standardized tests, criterion tests, and competency examinations by drilling children on the types of items found on tests, for example, recognizing correctly and incorrectly spelled words, choosing the appropriate vocabulary term, recognizing correctly punctuated sentences. Indeed, given the present climate of opinion, teachers might well be advised to provide concentrated practice in completing exercises of this kind during the weeks immediately preceding the test. But they should recognize that the time spent on practicing test-taking may contribute little to the improvement of writing ability, however important improved test scores may be in demonstrating to the public an increased rigor in the instructional program. Teach to the test then, if we cannot change the test, for six or eight weeks; and then fill the balance of the year's program with something more worthwhile.

Dealing with a Variety of Language Functions

A cluster of research studies during recent years has demonstrated how restricted are the varieties of language that traditionally have occupied the attention of formal instruction: a particular kind of creative writing, for example, in the intermediate grades, a concentration on personal and business letter writing, a single mode of expository writing in high school—a unique genre most often circumscribed by the demands of the college classroom. Rather than expand the child's experiences in using language in diverse ways, school programs have tended to limit the uses and thus the possibilities for growth.

Yet studies first by Michael Halliday and his followers in England, by James Britton, by Courtney Cazden, by Frank Smith, and by others have emphasized the substantial growth that results from planned experiences with many varieties of language.[8] There are many ways to describe the varieties of language that can be introduced in school programs, and each researcher develops a taxonomy. I prefer a highly practical focus on the uses of language through discrete operational categories: analyzing, reporting, persuading, interpreting, reflecting, imagining, inventing. However categorized, the need for providing variety in instructional uses of language is manifest.

Nor must all writing be done in the language arts curriculum. Young people need writing experiences in science and social science classrooms if they are to acquire the vocabulary and learn to command the language structures unique to each discipline. It may surprise some to learn that from the fifth grade onward, more writing occurs in science than in any content area (perhaps in as many as 50 percent of all science classes) because recording observations and reporting on laboratory experiences are part of the basic methodology. And because of the close interrelationship of reading and writing, one result of this emphasis seems to be that young people in high school have fewer problems in reading science books than in reading those written for other content areas. At least as a publisher, I encounter fewer requests in this area to write "down," to avoid technical vocabulary, to reduce the level of challenge of textbooks.

In the social sciences, where one informal study suggests that fewer than 25 percent of the classes require writing after the fifth grade, and in mathematics, where the percent may be closer to five, conditions are far different. Children who aren't asked to write in a discipline are denied the opportunity to learn the ways in which vocabulary and language structures interact in that discipline. One result is a demand for high school books written at low reading levels.[9] Small wonder that Jeanne Chall in her analysis of textbooks in relation to declining SAT scores expressed concern about the lack of challenge of many texts. Not only is the low reading level of these books a matter of concern, but so is the finding that few of them ask students to write.[10] And Chall's concern about the lack of writing applies to grammar and composition textbooks as well as to books in other subjects.

Distinguishing between the Composing Processes and Supportive Skills

An understanding of grammar; a knowledge of punctuation, capitalization, and the conventions of manuscript form; the mastery of discrete vocabulary terms—all these involve specific skills that can be acquired without improving the ability to write effective, coherent prose. Call them subskills. Call them enroute skills. Whatever the label, these skills need to be distinguished carefully from the basic composing processes—the ability to write an effective paragraph, say, or to sustain a point of view.

A basic skill, a subskill if you prefer, is for the most part acquired through instruction that emphasizes mastery learning—direct instruction, concentrated practice for short periods, criterion testing, second instruction, and a plan for maintenance.[11] Basic processes, on the other hand, are acquired only through growth models of learning extended over long periods of time. No one has yet mastered the ability to write a paragraph after six concentrated weeks of instruction! Improvement of basic processes occurs only over several years. In planning twelve-year programs to teach children to write, therefore, we need to distinguish between skills to be taught for mastery and processes to be taught for growth. Mastery of processes will be measured over a long period of time in relation to general improvement; mastery of specific skills will be achieved more rapidly and must, therefore, be taught for short-term accomplishment. To plan such a dual curricular sequence—skills for mastery, processes for growth— requires the identification of a limited number of skills to be mastered at every grade level, not more than thirty skills, say, given the thirty instructional weeks available in most schools and the need to provide practice if children are to achieve mastery. Children, for example, might learn the form for the personal letter once and then be held responsible for that knowledge. We would not then confuse mastery of the letter form with the effectiveness of what is written, an effectiveness that increases in complexity and richness with each passing year.

The confusion of skills and processes has to a considerable degree prevented us from planning effective programs. We have "exposed" children to a hundred different skills and processes each year from the third grade on. (Try, for example, to find any degree of agreement as to what a typical fourth-grader or eighth-grader might be expected to master in composition.) By separating skills and processes, however, we can apply many of the concepts of mastery learning without limiting our instruction to the obvious.

Identifying the Most Teachable Moments for Instruction

Although ways of viewing the processes of composing are many, consideration of what is most appropriately taught during the prewriting phase, the composing phase, and the postcomposing phase offers important clues to improving basic instruction.[12]

The precomposing phase is the period of invention and planning: helping young writers to acquire ideas by asking questions, suggesting basic crutches for planning—ways of paragraphing, outlining, using the topic sentence, encouraging students to consider point of view and audience. These, at appropriate levels, are important instructional emphases for those moments prior to writing.

An important instructional requirement of the second phase, the period of composing, is to arrange for substantial amounts of writing to be done in class when the teacher is present to assist the writers. The teacher who confines instruction in writing to assessments that occur after writing is completed works only with the improvement of product, not with the improvement of the process of writing. Such teachers know that a student has gone wrong, but they seldom know *why* that student has gone wrong. By moving around the class while writing occurs, the teacher can quickly identify students who need help, either on a group or an indiviual basis, and can provide that help at the time when it is most needed. Such teachers can help young writers to become reflective rather than reactive writers—to use the terms applied by Graves, who reports that as early as the first grade effective writers predict from four to ten sentences ahead what they plan to say.[13]

The postwriting phase is the period of editing, the time to emphasize those neglected skills that NAEP reports few American students have acquired even by the time they are seventeen years old. What we apparently do is to tell students to edit or revise, but we do not teach them how. Editing skills—improving content, organization, sentence structure, and the mechanics of a piece of writing—are acquired only as we plan carefully for young people to learn them. It is here, I think, that we suffer from a serious misinterpretation of the substantial body of research in English grammar that has demonstrated conclusively and correctly the lack of relationship between the study of grammar and improvement in ability to compose.[14] What we have failed to see clearly during these many years is that the very knowledge of the structure of English that contributes little to the improvement of writing is essential to the improvement of editing skills. Who can, after all, unlock the vagaries of a muddled sentence unless he or she can identify the essential elements of the sentence and the methods of expansion and modification? Basic insights into the structure of English, taught as part of the editing process and not in relation to composing, should and can have real meaning for students. In focusing our research attention on the relationship of grammar and writing, we may well have missed the essential connection.

There is much more that can be said about research, practice, and the improvement of instruction in writing, but the four points I have developed here suggest new priorities in themselves:

1. Sufficient time must be given to important tasks.
2. A variety of functions of language must be taught.
3. A distinction must be made between basic skills taught for mastery and basic processes taught for growth.
4. Teachable moments in which to introduce critical learning must be found before, during, and after the act of composing.

As this paper suggests, I see less a collision between present research and instructional trends than a redirection of both. The back-to-the-basics movement may well provide us with an opportunity to redefine our priorities and to focus more directly on the teaching of writing. It is just possible that we have become too doctrinaire about what to do and what not to do in helping children learn to write. If so, the current upheaval may well help us to modify and enlarge our perceptions.

Notes

1. See, for example, *Improving Educational Achievement* (Washington, D.C.: National Academy of Education, 1978).

2. *On Further Examination: Report of the Advisory Panel on the Scholastic Aptitude Test Score Decline* (New York: College Entrance Examination Board, 1977).

3. Scott Thomson and Nancy De Leonibus, *Guidelines for Improving SAT Scores,* ed. Thomas F. Koerner (Reston, Va.: National Association of Secondary School Principals, 1978).

4. James D. Koerner, ed., *The Teaching of Expository Writing* (New York: Alfred P. Sloan Foundation, 1978); Donald H. Graves, *Balance the Basics: Let Them Write* (New York: Ford Foundation, 1978); and *1969-1970, Writing: National Results* (Denver, Colo.: National Assessment of Educational Progress, 1970). See also *Write/Rewrite: An Assessment of Revision Skills* (Denver, Colo.: National Assessment of Educational Progress, 1977).

5. Arthur N. Applebee, *A Survey of Teaching Conditions in English, 1977* (Urbana, Ill.: National Council of Teachers of English, 1978).

6. Leo A. Munday, "Changing Test Scores and What They Mean, with Particular Emphasis on School Achievement since 1970" (Paper given to the Association of American Publishers, May 13, 1978).

7. See the discussion of these points in Graves, pp. 8, 10-11.

8. Peter Doughty, John Pearce, and Geoffrey Thornton, *Language in Use* (London: Edward Arnold, Schools Council Programme in Linguistics and English Teaching, 1971); James Britton, Tony Burgess, Nancy Martin, Alex McLeod, and Harold Rosen, *The Development of Writing Abilities (11-18),* Schools Council Research Studies (London: Macmillan Education, 1975); Courtney B. Cazden, Vera P. John, Dell Hymes et al., eds. *Functions of Language in the Classroom* (New York: Teachers College Press, 1972); and Frank Smith, "The Uses of Language," *Language Arts* 54 (September 1977): 638-44.

9. Donald Graves includes a discussion of this point in his report to the Ford Foundation cited earlier.

10. J. S. Chall, *An Analysis of Textbooks in Relation to Declining SAT Scores* (New York: The College Board, 1977).

11. Benjamin S. Bloom, *Human Characteristics and School Learning* (New York: McGraw-Hill Book Co., 1976).

12. Charles R. Cooper and Lee Odell adopt this division of the composing process in their helpful *Evaluating Writing: Describing, Measuring, Judging* (Urbana, Ill.: National Council of Teachers of English, 1977).

13. Donald Graves, "Children's Writing: Research Directions and Hypotheses Based upon an Examination of the Writing Processes of Seven-year-old Children" (Doctoral diss., State University of New York at Buffalo, 1973).

14. See Richard Braddock, Richard Lloyd-Jones, and Lowell Schoer, *Research in Written Composition* (Champaign, Ill.: National Council of Teachers of English, 1963); and "Back to the Basics: Grammar and Usage," *SLATE* 1, no. 3 (August 1976), published by the National Council of Teachers of English, Urbana, Illinois. Two studies with similar results are reported by Anthony R. Petrosky, "Grammar Instruction: What We Know," in *English Journal* 66 (December 1977): 86–88.

Some Principles of Composition
from Grade School to Grad School

E. D. Hirsch, Jr.
University of Virginia

I will be discussing some basic areas of composition that persist from the early grades to adult education. What I have to say will sometimes be speculative rather than final or definitive. I decided on this approach because I think a suggestive and speculative discussion is sometimes more useful than one in which the writer offers a package that is completely (and prematurely) wrapped up and tied with a ribbon. A former teacher of mine shrewdly advised me never to bother going to hear someone talk about the subject of a book the speaker had just finished writing. As author, he or she would be too busy defending the ideas in the book. Always invite a speaker, he said, who is still in the process of working out an idea and therefore is still open to new ideas and willing to change old ones. Accordingly, I will spare the reader a discussion of what I have said in my recent book on composition, and offer instead some ideas that I've been pondering—ideas about some very basic principles that might improve instruction in composition. The first can be stated as a simple question: Why is writing so difficult? Although I shall deal with some subsidiary questions, this, I think, is the most interesting and potentially useful idea I shall be discussing.

That writing *is* difficult no one will deny. The most practiced of professional writers tell us that writing is hard work—even those prolific persons, whom I so envy, who can type without looking at the keys. No matter how the words are set down, writing is at every level resistant to easy fluency, and at every stage of excellence a writer will sometimes find the going to be hard. Even Trollope, who started a new novel on the day he finished an old one, took pride in the difficulty, not the facility of his task. This point, so well-known to all of us from earliest schooling, is one of those important truths that are too obvious to be noticed. I take it up for special consideration because an understanding of the various reasons for the difficulty of writing may perhaps disclose some sound basic teaching principles.

To hear parents and politicians, not to mention colleagues, complain that present-day students cannot write clear, effective prose, one would think that the skill was a birthright of every citizen, or that the complainers themselves could all manage the skill easily. Behind the outcry over writing, there is, I suspect, a barely conscious uneasiness that one cannot write very well oneself. One knows secretly that writing is *very* hard, and its principles *very* uncertain—at least for oneself. An indication of this hidden uneasiness is the fervor with which we all hold strong feelings for and against words like *hopefully* and *insightful,* as though our lexical tastes had anything to do with the central skills of writing. Strong feelings about such trivia are probably a sign of our uncertainty about the basic principles that matter.

I have heard it proposed that the reason writing is more difficult to learn than reading or speaking is that students read and speak all the time, while they write only rarely. Consequently, it is lack of practice that makes the task so hard. No doubt that is partly right, but it cannot explain why writing was difficult for Anthony Trollope and has been for everyone else before or since. Clearly, it is not the act of writing—the motor skill—that makes the task eternally hard, though for unpracticed writers, lack of fluency in the motor skills multiplies the difficulties enormously. Writing is difficult, first of all, because it is an *inherently* more difficult mode of communication than ordinary speech.

The British linguist Randolph Quirk has in his laboratory a library of oral tapes that were recorded when the speakers were unaware that they were being taped, and these tapes when transcribed into writing are very often quite incomprehensible. Nowadays everybody knows this to be true of ordinary conversation—even of rather formal discussions—because in our time we have seen the printed transcripts of the Nixon tapes. These transcriptions hold hundreds of passages like this one:

> You see I'm, I'm just thinking it through on this one. It appeared to be forthcoming and that I wouldn't let the Dean thing be a fracas, if not necessary. I just think that that's one move you can make now at the present time. I just go—I think I'm a proponent of the idea that "buy a good headline for a day" and invite Dean back for later on. But we're going to get beat on the head and shoulders. Let's face it. We're going to get it until the Grand Jury indicts and then, that would be maybe another three weeks. After that, when they do indict, then they'll say, "Mr. President, what the hell are you going to hold Dean to the (unintelligible)?" I think we've got to do that. I just feel it's one of those things. To announce it, that I make it tomorrow night. Would you do that? To repudiate that today, you know, that means Tuesday.

When these words were spoken, they were immediately understand-able, but for us who read them, they are largely incomprehensible. Everyone recognizes why they are incomprehensible. It is because the speakers were in the midst of a situation familiar to them, but not to us. They could understand the spoken words even when they were brief and elliptical. In fact, it takes less effort on the part of both the speaker and the hearer to engage in brief and elliptical, rather than explicit, conversation, and the principle of least effort is one of the most firmly established principles of linguistics. In normal circum-stances, we would waste a great deal of our time and energy if we conversed so that what we said could later be understood from a written transcript. So, the first and basic reason why writing is dif-ficult is that it is an artificial speech-construct that demands a set of skills remote from ordinary conversational uses of language.

Let us imagine for a moment the kind of artificial situation in which we would have to speak as we must write. We would have to construct a barrier of some sort between ourselves and our listener so that we could not see him or her, so that we could not know whether there was one listener or many, so that we could not know their personalities or their responses. And on their side, they could not know anything in advance about us. No speaker ordinarily labors under these very deprived circumstances, whereas every writer does.

There is in the modern world one use of speech analogous to the situation that I have just described. It is a monologue delivered over the radio. In radio, unlike television, the speaker cannot be seen. He or she is a disembodied voice speaking to unseen, unfamiliar persons, as though a great barrier had been erected that only the voice could penetrate. I wonder how many people would be able to give a clear, coherent radio talk off the cuff? Certainly far fewer than could carry on a clear, coherent conversation face to face with another person. And if anyone *could* give a clear, coherent radio talk off the cuff, assuming that he or she had never done it before, we could be sure of one thing—that person *must* be a practiced writer.

Now it happens that we have evidence to support this conjecture, and it is found in the observations of the editors for a British journal, *The Listener*, a magazine composed mostly of talks given over BBC Radio, some of them spontaneous remarks in response to an inter-viewer. Most of these spontaneous monologues have very awkward patches in them, passages in which speakers realize they must back-track and explain after they recognize that the radio audience cannot nod or signal or see their facial expressions. The editors of *The Listener*, therefore, habitually do a lot of cutting and trimming and inserting in order to turn these radio monologues into acceptable writing. But there have been some exceptional BBC interviewees who do not require this editorial first aid, Germaine Greer, for instance. These persons are invariably practiced writers. Unaccustomed to radio delivery, these speakers are nonetheless used to the special constraints under which writers, like radio monologuists, must operate.

I have used radio as a nearer analogue to writing than oratory for a very basic reason. In writing you can never be sure *who* your audience will be. In speech making, in classroom lectures, in Sunday sermons, you speak in a concrete situation, before an audience that can nod, or look blank, or look skeptical, or laugh appreciatively—and you can adjust your delivery to that audience. In radio as in writing you cannot depend on these responses. For that reason, radio has developed the conventions of the live audience, and also the convention of canned laughter, so that listeners can pretend that they are part of a concrete situation rather than responders to the impersonal modulations of a loudspeaker. Writers have long deployed similar devices, particularly in the early days of writing; one example is the "live" audience of Chaucer's pilgrims. In short, writing has all of the difficulties of oratory and monologic utterance, plus the further difficulty of being a decontextualized utterance addressed to a vague audience. This double difficulty is, I think, the main source of the great difficulty of writing—it is both monologic speech and partly decontextualized speech. My point is that quite apart from the difficulties of learning the motor skills of penmanship and the mysteries of spelling and punctuation, writing is a kind of communication *inherently* more difficult than ordinary talk. Even when this kind of communication is oral, as on the radio, it is very difficult.

In ordinary talk, we assume a huge extent of prior understanding from our listeners—so much prior understanding that little strain is put on the linguistic vehicle. In fact, our listeners often understand what we are going to say before we have finished saying it. Only because of that do children learn how to speak at all; they first understand what we are saying by means other than words; then and only then are they able to understand what the words mean. The situation is very different, however, when we talk to strangers. They cannot be expected to understand what we mean almost before we speak our few elliptical words, and so we greatly expand and contextualize our speech, as we characteristically do in writing. A rather striking example of this social truth was recently reported in *Scientific American.*[1] In this first scene of the experiment we find the experimenter on the streets of Cambridge, Massachusetts, approaching a passerby. The experimenter, dressed like a native Cantabrigian in cap and tweed jacket, speaks with a distinct Boston accent and carries a copy of the *Boston Globe*. He asks, "How d'ya get to Central Square?" The passerby answers without breaking stride, using just five words that wouldn't count in many quarters as a complete sentence: "First stop on the subway." For this answer to be meaningful, consider some of the nonlinguistic knowledge the passerby assumed in the questioner: that the questioner knows where the subway is; that he knows which direction on the subway you go to find Central Square; that he doesn't expect or use the more elaborate forms of courtesy customary with complete strangers in less brusque and urban parts of the world. In the experiment, this little scene was enacted numerous times with similar results.

Now, in the next phase of the experiment, the experimenter dons boots, string tie, and western hat—all un-Cantabrigian clothes and prefaces his question with the statement, "I'm from out of town." Responses now were much elaborated, including explicit and involved instructions, descriptions of landmarks, and gestures. After a time, the experimenter found that he could get the same results if he merely announced his ignorance of local geography by adopting a rural Missouri accent, which is unusual enough in Cambridge to communicate quite clearly: "I'm from out of town."

Notice how much closer this second exchange is to the kind of discourse that we use in writing. Talking to strangers causes us to be much more explicit both in content and syntax. This particular example deviates from the requirements of writing mainly at the beginning of the reply. If, for instance, the local expert were asked to write out directions for a stranger who wanted to get from A to B, he or she could not say "You go down those stairs into the subway" but would be constrained into still greater explicitness, such as "At the corner of Boylston and Grantham Streets you'll see a blue sign labeled subway, and you go down the subway stairs, and then follow the red signs for the Quincey train." In this third case, the stranger is assumed to be ignorant not only of local geography but also of the intonations and gestures of the speaker. Consequently, even more explicit detail is required in the directions that are given in writing.

Now, the subjects of this experiment were all adults, not the very young people some of us are called on to instruct in the skill of writing. And the younger the child, the more difficult it is for the child to communicate with total strangers, and the more difficult therefore to learn the complex requirements of communication through writing. Piaget has taught us how difficult it is for very young children to imagine a stranger's point of view. But even past the age of eight, when extreme egocentrism has disappeared, children may still find it difficult to perform all the complex reckonings required in written communications. I mention the difficulties experienced by young children because their problems are extreme manifestations of the difficulties that are inherent in writing at every stage; children, therefore, provide us with an insight into the kinds of problems that must still be overcome by adults when they undertake to write. To this end, I'm going to describe another experiment—one performed by Sam Glucksberg and Robert Krauss—that shows in its simplest form the communicative complexity of writing.

In this experiment, a physical barrier is placed between two subjects so that communication must take effect, as in writing, through words alone. One subject's task is to describe to the other a series of six unfamiliar shapes so that the listener can identify and number them. Now describing these shapes to another person turned out to be a ridiculously easy task for adults. Even when only one subject was allowed to speak, the adult always managed to score one hundred percent on the very first try. The only noteworthy aspect of the experiment was that adults tended to be prolix in their descriptions. They understood that under the circumstances a lot of explicitness was required, though far, far less than would be needed if the other subject had had no illustrations to refer to. By contrast, when nursery school children were asked to put the six shapes in a given order, by putting blocks on a peg, they could not complete a single error-free trial because they used only the elliptical, idiosyncratic speech forms appropriate to talk with intimates at home.

The level of competence at this task—which approximates the writing task in obvious ways—has interesting correlations with age. Kindergartners perform *no* better than nursery school children and display the same lack of improvement with practice. First-, third-, and fifth-graders (this is highly surprising) were no better than kindergartners in their first trials. The older children did get better with practice, but even then, fifth-graders did not approach adult levels and seventh-graders did only about as well as fifth-graders. Even ninth-graders took seven to nine trials before they could begin to get perfect results consistently. Now, no one believes that a fourteen-year-old is linguistically incompetent or trapped in egocentrism. There is something about the nature of the task itself that creates difficulties that are seriously taxing to a young person. And the explanation suggested by Glucksberg and Krauss seems to me both persuasive and crucial—applicable to the teaching of writing at all levels.

In their view, the reason for the difficulty of communicative tasks similar to writing cannot lie in children's ignorance of what the task requires. Glucksberg has shown that when the demands of the task are very light, children communicate as successfully as adults do, using quite social and nonegocentric speech. It is only when the cognitive load of the task begins to get heavy that their performance begins to degenerate, even though they do possess the separate communicative skills that make up the complex task. They simply cannot bring all of them into play at once. Glucksberg and Krauss put their point this way:

> Even mature and articulate adults can find themselves in situations where they fail to take another person's knowledge and perspective into account. Consider the American tourist in a foreign country who asks, "Where is the men's room?" and on receiving no answer because his informant speaks no English, proceeds to shout, "Men's room, toilet, where?" Such an adult is not very different from the child who tries to communicate an unfamiliar geometric form by calling it "Daddy's shirt." Both the tourist and the child are ordinarily able to distinguish social from nonsocial speech and to communicate socially, and yet both may find themselves so overwhelmed by the demands of the particular situation that they do not bring that ability into play.[2]

Or to use the phrasing of information theory—the cognitive demands of the task cause a degeneration of performance because they *overload* a person's information-processing capacity.

Cognitive overload—the explanation put forward by Glucksberg and Krauss—seems to me a concept whose importance for writing instruction should be emphasized. Therefore, let me give a very brief account of the psychological principles behind it. The conception is based on the established truth that our cognitive faculties are very strictly limited in the number of things that we can pay attention to when we perform a complex task. In the terms of psychologists influenced by information theory, we all have a very limited channel capacity. To be precise, we can hold in our working memory only about five to seven discrete chunks of information, and this limitation on working memory means that we cannot perform tasks that require us to pay attention to ten or twelve aspects at once.

We can and do perform tasks that have many more than ten or twelve aspects, but we cannot do this if all the aspects are unfamiliar ones which require attention simultaneously. That would be like learning tennis from a book, and in the space of a single stroke attending to the following:

1. Turn sideways.
2. Shift weight to rear foot.
3. Change to forehand grip.
4. Bring racket back low.
5. Keep a stiff wrist.
6. Keep your eye on the ball.
7. Let your arm lead your body.
8. Shift weight from rear to front.
9. Swing from the shoulder.
10. Swing through the ball.
11. Swing from low to high.
12. Finish with racket aimed at net.
13. Hit the ball down the line.
14. Keep the racket face open.
15. Let your rear foot move towards the front.
16. Use a relaxed swing.
17. Bend your knees.
18. Keep your shoulders on a level with the ball.

Here I'll stop, because you have taken the point, but, as almost everyone knows, this list could be much extended. And another thing you know is that if you try to attend to all of these imperatives, you will hit a *terrible* stroke, one worse than if you had concentrated on just one or two rules. In short, when we overload our channel capacity, our performance is worse than usual, even for subtasks that we can perform well by themselves.

Now we know that this principle applies to the skill of writing because of work by Fred Godshack and his colleagues and, more recently, by Ellen Nold and Sarah Freedman.[3] If you give students a composition topic that is *easy* for them, their sentences will be more varied and coherent; their spelling, and even their punctuation, will be better than it would be on a topic that is difficult for them. In other words, if you tax the channel capacities of students by the demands of the topic, you overload their circuits, and you degrade all aspects of their performances: ideas, diction, spelling, syntax. So strong is this effect of topic variance that Godshack required students to write on five different topics before he drew a judgment about their writing skills per se.

This conception of cognitive overload and its operation in writing powerfully supports the conjectures drawn by Mina Shaughnessy in her work on the writing of intelligent but untrained adults in remedial college courses. If you're concerned about your spelling, how can you attend to ideas, and if you're concerned about spelling and ideas, how can you pay attention to style? Attending to all these things at once can make an intelligent student appear simpleminded. And if, in addition, you must also recognize the very special communicative difficulties of written speech, the task is intimidating indeed. Small wonder, then, that untrained students write with a brevity and ineptness that belie their understanding of the subject. Here is an example from one of Shaughnessy's students: "Yes, being that today's jobs are being made impossible to get without a college degree with the, to high school graduates."[4] And here is a poignant example of the way cognitive overload contributes to writer's block—in the following starts again by one of Shaughnessy's students.

Start 1: Seeing and hearing is something beautiful and strange to infant.

Start 2: To a infant seeing and hearing is something beautiful and stronge to infl

Start 3: I agree that seeing and hearing is something beautiful and stronge to a infants. A infants heres a strange sound such as work mother, he than acc

Start 4: I agree that child is more sensitive to beauty, because its all so new to him and he apprec

Start 5: The main point is that a child is more sensitive to beauty than there parents, because its the child a inftant can only express it feeling with reactions,

Start 6: I agree a child is more senstive to seeing and hearing than his parent, because its also new to him and more appreciate. His

Start 7: I agree that seeing and hearing have a different quality for infants than grownup, because when infants comes aware of a sound and can associate it with the object, he is indefeying and the parents acknowledge to to this

Start 8: I agree and disagree that seeing and hearing have a different quality for infants than for grownups, because to see and hear for infants its all so new and mor appreciate, but I also feel that a child parent appreciate the sharing

Start 9: I disagree I feel that it has the same quality to[5]

The way Shaughnessy interprets these and other examples from inexperienced adult writers seems to me absolutely right, in view of Krauss and Glucksberg's work. Shaughnessy conjectures that these examples do not reflect paucity of intelligence or knowledge or imagination but do reflect the halting efforts of inexperience and intimidation before the problems of spelling and grammar. In short, having to pay attention to so many things at once degrades *every* aspect of performance so that highly intelligent adults can produce writing that is virtually unintelligible. We can take this point still further.

The chief problems in teaching writing—certainly to youngsters after the age of ten—are fairly similar at all grade levels. This statement implies that the appropriate psychological model for teaching composition after that age is not a model of developmental psychology but one of skill acquisition, where the problems of the sixth-grader are not different in principle from the problems of the inexperienced college freshman.

If the problem of cognitive overload is a universal problem at all levels of writing experience, what can the teacher do to improve performance most rapidly? Or to put the question another way: How can the composition teacher most effectively help students reduce the excessive cognitive demands of writing? Well, I'm not daring or foolish enough to suggest a monolithic or pat answer, but I do think we can deduce some principles that will be useful for any age group and any level of writing experience.

There are two basic ways to reduce cognitive overload. One is to make certain aspects of the task automatic, so that those aspects take up little or none of our very limited channel capacity. These skills thereby become second nature and are relegated to some portion of the mind well away from the foreground of consciousness. The second is to subdivide the task itself so that only a part of it occupies our attention at any one time.

If we look at the practice of highly expert writers, we find that they employ both of these techniques, though often in very different ways. Since expert writers will have already automated the obviously repeatable subskills of writing, like spelling and typing and handwriting, most of their tricks will be directed to subdividing their task. They will tend to work out their general strategy before they write their first sentences, whether or not they use an outline. But most of all, they will have learned how to leave certain details to a later stage, so that they won't have to bother with those details at the moment. Researchers like Linda Flower and John Hayes are investigating this whole question of what expert writers actually do when they write,[6] but before their results are in, we can safely predict two findings: (1) Expert writers will do different things, and (2) their various techniques will turn out to be methods of task-subdivision that will reduce the cognitive load at any given moment in the writing process. Chief among these parceling techniques will of course be techniques of revision.

But for very young writers, and others without much experience, it seems to me that the huge cognitive demands of writing must be reduced first of all by automating the technical and repeatable skills— even if that means, as Shaughnessy suggests, that we encourage some of these people to learn typing as soon as possible. Other recurrent and repeatable skills will involve such communicative peculiarities of writing as the need to be long-winded and explicit and the need to focus on one thing at a time—and other general principles for communicating to strangers. To encourage fluency and automation in these skills, it would seem prudent for teachers to limit the intellectual demands of the assigned topic a good deal of the time. But I think it is much wiser for the teacher to understand the general principles than to follow a rigid plan. Until we have a lot more reliable information about what works best for different groups, sound principles (such as the principle of reducing the cognitive load) are going to be more useful than rigidly specific teaching methods.

If the principle of cognitive overload is as important as I think it is for the teacher of writing, then the back-to-basics movement contains an intuitive wisdom that some educationists have regarded with insufficient humility. One meaning of back to basics in writing is an emphasis on spelling and penmanship, along with correct grammatical and lexical usage. Opponents to this movement praise the superior virtues of prewriting techniques, of syntactic fluency, and, in some cases, of self-expression. But there is a false division in these camps, if we follow the principle of cognitive overload as a psychological principle. For it may be the case (and I think it very likely) that the fastest road to syntactic fluency is through the repetitive and apparently rigid imposition of spelling and penmanship standards and grammatical and lexical usage.

My speculation follows this logic: Spelling and penmanship, like lexical and grammatical norms, are scribal conventions that are present in every piece of writing. Since they are ever present, they are primary candidates for automation in the skill of writing, in order that they do not have to occupy any of the mental space that is needed for thinking about the topic or about the strategy of presentation. The more these scribal conventions are automated, the more the mind is free to devote itself to fluent writing. That is why correctness is no enemy to fluency and self-expression, but rather their close ally and bosom friend. No matter when the scribal conventions are learned— whether in remedial college writing courses for adults or in elementary school—the conventions *do* need to be automated sometime in order to free the mind for complex and variable tasks. That is the implicit wisdom in the back-to-basics movement among parents, so far as writing is concerned.

Moreover, my very limited experience tells me that the dull grind of memorization in spelling and usage, the dull repetitions of motor skills, are anything but dull to younger children. They *like* limited tasks that they can master, and they revel in their mastery. They like to memorize. I would not be surprised if they took more pleasure in mastering the repeatable scribal conventions of writing than in a steady diet of imaginative writing that is heedless of correctness. It is at least possible that we have overromanticized the wisdom and completeness of the hidden soul of the child as expressed in imaginative writing. And even if that is not true, we have surely overestimated the value of writing in developing that hidden soul. Writing is a very inappropriate tool of self-discovery. It is an inefficient form of speaking to an intimate or to one's self. If writing were self-expression, then the child in Krauss and Glucksberg's study who described one of the designs as "Daddy's shirt" would have provided as good a description as the adult who said "a spaceman's helmet." But in fact, "Daddy's shirt" was not as good. Writing is really antipathetic to self-expression and to inner speech. It is a very public form of communication. That is one of the most basic basics of writing, as the Glucksberg-Krauss experiments showed.

Indeed, my experience as a writing teacher makes me draw from those experiments an inference that extends and qualifies the overload theory of Glucksberg and Krauss. While it is true that the cognitive demands of speaking to unseen strangers are great enough to tax a young child's mind, it is also true that repeated failures by fourteen-year-olds suggest difficulties in addition to cognitive overload. Their failures also suggest a deficiency of social-cultural knowledge. Highly socialized adults know what to say across the experimental barrier because they know what knowledge and associations can be assumed in an adult partner. Writers must similarly have a good idea of what an audience already knows, else they would need to be endlessly explicit—or risk communicative failure. Much of what is conveyed by any piece of writing is inexplicit. Hence writing, like conversation, is elliptical; it is simply much less extremely so. Writing depends not just on shared linguistic conventions between reader and writer, but also on a vast domain of shared cultural knowledge that few children can have acquired before age fifteen or sixteen. That is another, powerful reason for stressing spelling, punctuation, and the joys of mere scribal fluency in younger children.

Nonetheless, the public and artificial quality in writing is a basic principle that we can also follow and develop all the way from grade school to grad school. Soon after children learn how to form words in script, they need to learn how very much more must be said in writing than in speech. Even the most highly skilled writers constantly remind themselves of that basic truth. We do not *think* the way we must write, and the connection between clarity of writing and clarity of thought has been overstated. When we think or talk to intimates, we juggle many balls in the air at once. When we write, we must follow an artificial rule to which there is no exception. It is the rule of one thing at a time. We must not move to another thing until that one thing can be at least vaguely understood by our reader. This rule governs other forms of communication of course. It is a basic principle in all forms of public, monologic utterance, and all competent public monologues exhibit it. If the paragraph did not exist, the deprivations of writing and of other speech-to-strangers would force us to invent it.

Let me illustrate this with one last example that makes a nice contrast with my first one—the excerpt from the Nixon tapes. It is the first stanza of a country song that I heard a few days ago on the radio, as sung by Linda Ronstadt. I'm not sure that I remember the words with absolute accuracy, but in folk art some variation is acceptable. Here's the way I remember the stanza:

> I'll never be married,
> I'll be no man's wife,
> I 'spect to live single
> All the days of my life.

Now, I would want to argue against the logical purist who might say that this stanza is just so much padding because there is nothing in lines two, three, and four that wasn't already in line one. On the contrary, repetition is its great virtue as a stanza and as a piece of writing. It illustrates in an especially pure form the truth discovered by Richard Meade and W. Geiger Ellis about the characteristic form of the paragraph in professional writing.[7] The normal paragraph consists of a set of sentences that *seem* to be developing an idea but are in fact repeating an idea from different angles and with different means. Writing has to do that, all public speech has to do that, because strangers cannot know just what you mean unless they get the meaning from several convergent angles. A folk singer knows this as well as any writer knows it.

And lastly, every *reader* also knows it in his or her bones. This mention of the reader introduces my final observation about the basics of writing. It takes a reader to make a writer. Nobody can write better than he or she can read, for we must all read our own writing even as we produce it. The techniques of explicitness and correctness that are peculiar to written speech can only become second nature to a person for whom reading is second nature. It therefore makes sense to consider reading as basic to writing, and even to include reading in a writing course if such instruction seems useful. In view of this, and in view of my example from Linda Ronstadt, it seems to follow that literature, and reading, and writing are a single subject rather than three subjects. Just as a folk song is writing, so is a technical essay on literature. Literature and reading and writing make up one world of literacy. And literacy is a larger and more important world than any of its components. We teachers of literacy are unwisely separated from each other in the separate domains of literature, reading, and writing. I think that is also a basic principle that remains valid from grade school to grad school.

Notes

1. Robert M. Krauss and Sam Glucksberg, "Social and Nonsocial Speech," *Scientific American* 236 (February 1977): 100–105.

2. Krauss and Glucksberg, pp. 104–5.

3. Fred I. Godshack et al., *The Measurement of Writing Ability* (New York: College Entrance Examination Board, 1966); and Ellen Nold and Sarah W. Freedman, "An Analysis of Readers' Responses to Essays," *Research in the Teaching of English* 11 (Fall 1977): 164–74.

4. Mina P. Shaughnessy, *Errors and Expectations: A Guide for the Teacher of Basic Writing* (New York: Oxford University Press, 1977), p. 221.

5. Shaughnessy, p. 7.

6. Linda S. Flower and John R. Hayes, "Problem-Solving Strategies and the Writing Process," *College English* 39 (December 1977): 449–61.

7. Richard A. Meade and W. Geiger Ellis, "Paragraph Development in the Modern Age of Rhetoric," *English Journal* 59 (February 1970): 219–26.

The Basics and the Imagination

James E. Miller, Jr.
University of Chicago

A few weeks ago as I was standing in a long line at the local bank waiting my turn and trying to imagine what I might write about for this conference, an elderly black gentleman standing in front of me turned suddenly and asked me point-blank: "Are you a senior citizen?" Needless to say, I was taken aback by the question, and being a teacher my first impulse was to ask him to define his terms. But I repressed that impulse and considered: Was I, indeed, a senior citizen? I might as well confess that deep down I resented the question and contemplated a bouncy, flip reply like, "Well, you know, you are as young as you feel." But as I floundered for an answer, the elderly gentleman pulled out a card to demonstrate that he was a card-carrying member of Senior Citizendom. He was, he told me proudly, seventy-two years old, and what he wanted to know was whether I knew about the discount given to senior citizens on a specific busline. With some relief, I told him no, I did not have such a card, and I did not know about the arrangements on the particular busline he mentioned. He chatted on about how he was enjoying retirement, while I mulled over the startling question he had posed. Was I a senior citizen? And somehow the question became muddled in my mind with the subject I had been meditating before it was posed—the basics and the imagination. Indeed, all my thought about the subject had gravitated to the past, and not just the recent past, but the distant past, the past so distinctly past that many young teachers today would have lived through it only as they babbled away in their playpens. The issues that lay behind my title and my topic were issues that gave me a fanciful sense of *déjà vu*, a strange feeling that I had somehow ended up where I had begun, and instead of knowing the place for the first time, was as baffled as before, and more battered.

I am going to begin my comments, then, by a look at the past that I have lived through, in an attempt to get the present in perspective.

But to allay your fears that you have fallen into the grip of some half-mad ancient mariner with a long yarn to spin. I shall tell you now that I have strictly limited my visit into the past to the first part of my commentary. My talk is divided into three parts: sifting through the debris, scanning the horizon, and re-excavating the foundations. After I had decided on these three sections, I realized that they represent an elaborated metaphor that connects my experience of the recent past: the earthquake that hit Guatemala shortly after 3 a.m. on February 4, 1976. That surrealistic morning I was wakened from a strange dream to the violent rocking of the house, and my memory of the aftermath of the earthquake might well be suggested by my section titles. It is not my intention to discuss the Guatemalan earthquake, but I am haunted by how I unconsciously connected a subject involving the state of our profession with my experiences following the earthquake. I shall not try to explain this connection, as I am not sure I understand it myself, but I shall hang on to the section titles because for me they have an authentic ring and because they may suggest what the profession at large needs somehow to undertake.

Sifting through the Debris

It was over two decades ago that an almost universal chorus went up from colleges and universities: "Back to the basics." The occasion was the Russian launching of Sputnik in 1957. Back in that pastoral period, questions were straightforward and answers simple. The question was simply who and what were to blame for the deficiencies of American education. The answer was, obviously, the schools of education. Devoted to the ideas of John Dewey and his concept of progressive education, they had trained teachers to ignore the basics in favor of greater and greater amounts of trivia in the curriculum. The solution was to force the basics (the basic subject matters, including history, mathematics, and English) back into the curriculum, even if that meant English, math, and history departments taking over the functions of schools of education.

It was back in that innocent time that I first became involved with the problems of teachers of English. As chair of the Department of English at the University of Nebraska, I suddenly found myself visiting high schools to discover what actually went on in English classrooms. My most vivid memory goes back to a visit to the Omaha schools. The English teachers had seized the occasion of my visit to complain of their problems. The first complaint was that they were being forced to graduate nonreaders from high school. I asked what they meant by nonreaders. They explained, suppressing their impatience, that they meant students who were not able to read. I expressed shock that such students were allowed to graduate. And they then pointed out to me that not only did the nonreaders graduate, but they were admitted to the University of Nebraska on fancy football scholarships. At this point I became more cautious in my questions. But soon they were talking about the difficulties of distributing nonbooks to their classes. I ignored the term for a while, but finally was unable to avoid asking what they meant by nonbooks. Again suppressing their impatience, they explained that the supply of school texts had diminished over the years through loss, theft, and destruction, but that the school administration, not wanting to face the expense of replacement, ignored this loss and forced teachers to continue to carry the nonbooks on their inventories—and to distribute them to their classes. It was then that I made the suggestion for which I am still remembered in Omaha: that the nonbooks be distributed to the nonreaders.

The classroom English teachers contributed more to my education than I did to theirs in these visits, and I soon discovered that there were no easy solutions to the problems of teaching English. Moreover, I discovered that high school teachers were not *them* but *us*. We had taught them in our classrooms, and it was our ideas and values that they in some measure reflected as they went about doing their jobs. But they had much to contend with—nonreaders and nonbooks as well as various kinds of community pressure, censorship, and indifference and various levels of administration stupidity, ignorance, and deviousness. Reform in education, it became clear quite early, would require more than the battle cry, "Back to the basics."

For those who lived through the reform years following Sputnik, the times were exciting and the possibilities seemed limitless. Solutions were popping out all over the country, and the Great Solution seemed just around the corner. Summer workshops, financed by the government or by foundations, were sponsored by English departments to retrain teachers. Curriculum centers came into being, undertaking to rewrite the curriculum from kindergarten to freshman English. Meetings and conferences were held, and manifestoes issued. The National Council of Teachers of English and even the more staid and aloof Modern Language Association became deeply involved in trying to shape the English curriculum. I remember earnest discussions about whether we should put *War and Peace* at the eleventh- or twelfth-grade level, about whether *Paradise Lost* (or part of it) would be suitable for a unit on myth in the ninth or tenth grade. Linguistics seemed in a permanent state of revolution, with new grammars making their appearance and then suddenly disappearing as still newer grammars came out. Publishers planned series of texts and changed them in midstream. There were great expectations for structural linguistics and generative grammar, and strange and mystic formulae were embedded in school texts to baffle both teachers and students. Composition, that rather clumsy third leg of what had come to be known as the sacred tripod of English (literature, language, composition), seemed less responsive to new approaches; nevertheless, new ways of teaching writing were proposed, some involving the variations and elaborations on the kernel sentence, others on the careful calculation and counting of clauses and phrases.

There was about a decade of such activity before the convening of the Anglo-American Conference on the Teaching and Learning of English at Dartmouth in the summer of 1966. But more than reform in English education had taken place in that decade in America. A social revolution was in progress; the civil rights movement was making itself felt everywhere, especially in the schools, and tensions were growing over Vietnam. The Dartmouth Conference, like Sputnik a decade before, may be taken as one of the turning points in our profession, not necessarily because of its documented influence but because of its symbolic impact on the participants and the profession. The Americans went to the Dartmouth Conference ladened with the curriculum materials and new texts they had been developing over the decade, confident that they would be able to help their British cousins who had been late-starters in the reform movement.

To the Americans, the British sounded like the progressive educationists with whom the Americans had been doing battle for a decade. To the British, the Americans must have sounded like the conservative academicians with whom the British had been doing battle for a similar period. The opening question to be decided was, What is English? Instead of the early agreement everyone expected, the question was set aside as too controversial and finally unanswerable. The Americans had confidently proposed that English, as a school subject, was simply—language, literature, and composition. The British pointed out that such a definition immediately determined the curriculum and centered it in subject matter, whereas they wished to center it in the student. The British, generally representing the new comprehensive schools in England, appeared more unified in their position than the Americans, and they repeatedly came back to two figures as points of reference: F. R. Leavis and D. H. Lawrence. They all seemed to be in some sense Leavisites, and they were unstinting in their praise of the effectiveness of Lawrence's fiction in the classroom.

It was clear that the group of Americans was more polyglot in its makeup and less unified in its opinions; and though the Americans had read both Leavis and Lawrence, they did not see how the two represented salvation for English education. I remain to this day perplexed as to how it was that the elitist, sometimes brilliant, sometimes paranoid, F. R. Leavis was transmogrified into the John Dewey of British education.

Needless to say, the British barely glanced at the elaborate curriculum materials: they sniffed around them, and on occasion picked out a page displaying incredibly intricate formulae purporting to explain principles of generative grammar and asked if we Americans *really* foisted this material off on our students. Few Americans volunteered to defend the material ridiculed by the British. As the Dartmouth Conference continued, the British and the Americans found that there were some subjects they could jointly explore without immediate division. And there was, in fact, some give-and-take. Many of the Americans, for example, came to the conference committed to excellence, and therefore committed to tracking—ability grouping that enabled the bright to move ahead without being held back by the intellectually handicapped or disadvantaged. The British, on the other hand, were unified in their opposition to streaming (again, ability grouping) because the streams tended to coincide with social classes and to inflict psychological damage on those placed in the lower streams. By the end of the conference there was general agreement that some tracking or streaming might be useful, but never when it was likely to reflect or imply class or racial discrimination and when psychological harm would outweigh educational advantage. From the beginning of the Dartmouth Conference it had been agreed that two books, one British and the other American, would be written out of the experience. Their titles suggest the basic differences that divided the two groups. The American book, by Herbert J. Muller, was called *The Uses of English;* the British book, by John Dixon, *Growth through English.*[1]

There was no doubt more movement beneath the surface at Dartmouth than in the open. It took some time, more than four weeks of the conference, for the participants to recover from the cultural shock of finding themselves so far from agreement. But I do not think it too much to say that the conference injected a healthy self-skepticism into the American scene. Less confidence was invested in a comprehensive curriculum based on language, literature, and composition, and more interest was aroused in the potentialities of a curriculum related to stages in student growth.

But the Dartmouth Conference was not the only motive for change during this period. American society had moved from the Age of Sputnik to the Age of Social Revolution. The live question in the schools seemed less frequently to be how to achieve excellence and more frequently how to achieve literacy. A K–13 English curriculum emphasizing excellence that had some success in an affluent suburb turned out to have little relevance in a ghetto school. Whatever the various causes, after Dartmouth it was no longer possible to be so hopeful that the profession's problems would be solved by the creation of a New English that would work the miracles that the New Math seemed to be working in a sister discipline.

In preparing my comments, I have sifted through some of the debris of my own professional past, looking over speeches and lectures I prepared during the time I was serving on the executive committee of the National Council of Teachers of English in the late 1960s and the early 1970s. I was surprised by the tone of the opening paragraphs of the speech I delivered in Washington, D. C., as president-elect of NCTE. I did not realize at the time how far I had traveled from the days of Sputnik, how far in the past lay the obvious solutions to a simple return to the basics. Listen and recall:

> Everywhere we look, the world is in a state of crisis. Every day the headlines bring us the latest disasters—assassination, starvation, riot, war. We live in fear and panic. The very earth itself, once a symbol of durability and stability, appears daily threatened: the skies close in on us with their brilliant poisons; the lands store up the pesticides to send back to us in our foods; the waters of our lakes and rivers, long used as sewers of our industries, become brackish and foul, and turn from refuge into menace. Birds drop listlessly from the trees, squirrels and other land creatures stagger with a strange lethargy, fish turn over on their sides and float aimlessly on the tops of the waters. In the midst of all this pollution, our students crowd into our classrooms, their throats rasping and their eyes watering from the acrid air, and we teachers ask them to rise and sing "America the Beautiful."
>
> But more dismaying than the pollutants contaminating our air, lands, and waters are those poisoning our souls. Young men are sent to distant lands to fight and die for democracy and freedom that they themselves have never known. Television screens bring the violence, agony, and torture of war daily into our comfortable living rooms and we become bored with the monotony of death. Presidential commissions issue reports without cease informing us that we are becoming two unequal nations, black and white; that our police forces in our cities throughout the land often victimize minority groups, and themselves sometimes riot against the citizenry, using all their superiority of strength and weaponry; that our courts do not hand out justice with impartiality, but interpret the law to favor the white and the rich; that our

schools, some fifteen years after the Supreme Court order to desegregate, remain segregated and unequal. The symbol of our poisoned souls may be the television close-up of the twisted, warped adult face—some mother's face—glaring and twitching with hate as an innocent black child marches bravely to school. And we teachers ask this and our other students to rise and pledge allegiance to an "indivisible" nation which promises "liberty and justice for all." [2]

These opening words of my address may seem strident to those who did not directly experience the social stresses and strains, the disruptions and eruptions, of the 1960s. But those who were involved remember the times as very dark indeed, fundamentally changing the ways we, as individuals, saw ourselves as Americans, and the ways we, as English teachers, conceived our professional role in society. My speech was entitled "The Linguistic Imagination" and, as its title implies, was not directed in its entirety to the social scene. Suffice it to say here, however, that in this sifting through the rubble of more than two decades of reform and change in English education, I discovered few items left intact. There are broken bits and pieces, including fragments of those very "basics" to which we had committed ourselves with passion. By definition, I imagine, basics cannot be smashed because they *are* basic. But there they are, shattered and in pieces. And thus I can only conclude that what we had proclaimed as the basics really were not basic in any authentic sense. When I now hear the cry "Back to the basics," I cannot help but remember this recent history and its sad fate.

Scanning the Horizon

It is good for a time to stop sifting through the debris, to walk up on a grassy slope, and to lift one's eyes to the horizon. What dangers lie there out of sight? What help might be on its way? I can speak only of the horizons I perceive from the center I occupy, and the signs I see are not reassuring. Organizations that a few years ago seemed to be attempting rescue missions regularly now seem to have retrenched, concentrating on their own survival.

University departments of English appear disoriented, their attention fixed on declining enrollments in their undergraduate literature courses and the disappearance of jobs for their new Ph.D.'s. Institutions preoccupied with their own survival are not likely to find time to concern themselves about the difficulties of others. Is it possible that departments of English, since they are not part of the solution, are part of the problem?

There has always been a curious gap between departments of English in the universities and English departments and language arts programs in the secondary and elementary schools. Traditionally, departments of English have handed over by default the responsibility for thinking about the teaching of their subject to departments and schools of education. The more prestigious the department of English, the less likely it was to be involved in thinking about the role of literature and language in education in elementary and high schools.

There may one day come a time when departments of English conceive of themselves not as separate and independent entities but as an integral part of the educational process in English that begins in the kindergarten. There may come a time when members of departments of English conceive as their colleagues not only their fellow department members but also their fellow English teachers who struggle with similar problems on the high school and elementary levels. There may come a time when teachers and professors of English at all levels of the curriculum—kindergarten through graduate school—discover their mutual interests and problems, come together in the joint enterprise of defining what is genuinely basic to their subject and discipline, and proceed to the construction of a curriculum centered in the truly basic.

But that time is not yet. And in the meantime, with departments of English under seige and concerned for their own survival, that time seems more distant than ever before. On the other hand, times of trial are often times of reorientation, times of reconsideration of old questions. There are faint signs that departments of English, in casting about for means of survival, may discover their responsibilities for their discipline and its role at all levels of education, and in the process recognize a mutuality of interest with colleagues working to the same ends at other levels of the curriculum.

In casting a cold eye on the horizon, we might note recent movements in literary criticism to see whether we can detect help from that direction. For anyone who tries to keep up with new critical movements, the times are very confusing; one movement is no sooner established in a stronghold when another appears to challenge it and do battle. It seems almost as though the interest in criticism these days is not in the excitement of discoveries universally recognized as basic principles but rather in the zest for linguistic combat in which one critical theory is pitted against another. I shall not attempt a systematic survey of the critical scene but will concentrate on a few examples of what I mean.

My first example I take from the recent past. Northrop Frye's archetypal criticism has been around long enough for us to have accommodated ourselves to it. Indeed, I remember that some of the curriculum centers of yesteryear committed themselves fully to the categories and methods outlined in Frye's book, *The Anatomy of Criticism* (1957); and Frye himself became involved with the educational implications of his system. I do not wish here to judge Frye's system, but I do wish to call into question one of the widely quoted principles that he formulated about the impossibility of "teaching literature": "The difficulty often felt in 'teaching literature' arises from the fact that it cannot be done: the criticism of literature is all that can be directly taught."[3] I think I know what led Frye to this conclusion, but I wonder whether he considered what the educational consequences of such a principle would be if actually adopted in a place such as an elementary classroom.

I would guess Frye thought that what could be taught directly was a body of knowledge or set of principles, and that since literature could not be reduced to such a body or set, it could not be taught. What I think he overlooked was that the classroom is a place of immense possibilities when presided over by a creative teacher. Such a teacher can create an emotional, intellectual, and imaginative environment in which a poem, play, or story *can* be experienced (and therefore learned) directly. The best teaching of a poem may, on occasion, be an effective reading of it; the best teaching of a play, a recreation of its scenes in the classroom, with full participation of the students in cast and audience. In any event, the teaching of literature need not be limited to the *talking about*—or criticism—of literature.

Since Frye we have witnessed the advent of the French structuralists and, more recently, the Yale deconstructionists. The works of these critics have brought into being a swarm of critical terms that often seem to obscure more than they clarify. Teachers trying to find a base from which they can confidently make plans for the classroom and wanting to connect this base with a professional center that they can look to for guidance will find little reassurance in the vocabularies of these new criticisms. It seems fair to conclude that many modern critical theorists have not only cut themselves off from a general audience, but from most of their fellow professionals, whom they are presumably most interested in reaching.

I do not wish to pass judgment wholesale on the bewildering variety of structuralists and deconstructionists, but merely to observe the apparent willingness with which they write for an ever shrinking

audience. Because I have recently read for other purposes several of
the books of Harold Bloom, I shall use his criticism as an example of
the trend I am tracing. Bloom can be called neither a structuralist nor
a deconstructionist (though at Yale he has affinities with the latter),
but a kind of Freudian Cabalist. The work that sets forth his critical
system most fully and explicitly is *The Anxiety of Influence: A Theory
of Poetry* (1973); but it needs to be supplemented by *A Map of
Misreading* (1975), elaborating his theory that a strong misreading (or
misprision) is the best misreading; and his *Wallace Stevens: The
Poems of Our Climate* (1977), filling out in an appendix (or "coda")
his theory of "poetic crossing" (in which a poet confronts successively
the death of creativity, of love, and of the total being by successively
crossing from irony to synecdoche, from metonymy to hyperbole, and
from metaphor to metalepsis).[4]

I shall not attempt to explain the whole of Bloom's system, but I
would like to list the categories he sets forth in *The Anxiety of
Influence.* As poets write poems in response to the works of predecessor poets, all poems may be seen as relating to prior poems in a
particular way, and would fit in one of the following categories
(which are really stages of reaction to or misreadings of predecessor
poems): Clinamen, or poetic misreading; Tessera, "completion and
antithesis"; Kenosis, "movement towards discontinuity with the precursor"; Daemonization, "movement towards a personalized Counter-
Sublime"; Askesis, "movement of self-purgation"; Apophrades, or
"return of the dead," wherein the new poem makes it seem "as
though the later poet himself had written the precursor's characteristic
work."[5] In connection with Apophrades, Bloom devotes straight-faced
and serious discussion, cleverly designed to shock, to the influence of
Wordsworth on Milton, Wallace Stevens on Keats, and Hart Crane
on Whitman.[6]

If I have already succeeded in losing or confusing you, don't be
discouraged. It would seem that most of Bloom's readers, like his
reviewers, have trouble comprehending or remembering his system,
and they wonder at times whether his formulations are not intended
to startle more than to convince. In what he calls an "Interchapter" in
The Anxiety of Influence, he writes: "Rhetorical, Aristotelian, phe-
nomenological, and structuralist criticisms all reduce, whether to
images, ideas, given things, or phonemes. Moral and other blatant
philosophical or psychological criticisms all reduce to rival conceptu-
alizations. We [the editorial "we"] reduce—if at all—to another
poem. The meaning of a poem can only be another poem." And
again: "Every poem is a misinterpretation of a parent poem. A poem

is not an overcoming of anxiety, but is that anxiety. Poets' misinterpretations or poems are more drastic than critics' misinterpretations or criticism, but this is only a difference in degree and not at all in kind. There are no interpretations but only misinterpretations, and so all criticism is prose poetry." [7] A teacher searching for support among these sentences before entering the classroom to confront the students' question, "What does this poem mean?" might understandably be hesitant in quoting Bloom: "Oh, the meaning of that poem is another poem." Who can blame such a teacher for turning back to Brooks and Warren and their durable textbook, first published in 1938, *Understanding Poetry*. With all its shortcomings—and new ones are being detailed and disclosed daily—the old New' Criticism lent itself to adaptation in the classroom; it did not set itself forth as a private cult with a patented vocabulary, bent on exclusivity.

Scanning the horizon cannot be terribly comforting for anyone looking for a new critical system that might serve as a rallying point for the teaching of literature through all the school years, a system that might bring the present fragments of the profession together into some kind of understandable whole, infusing the enterprise with a sense of purpose and even mission. Indeed, some of the new systems seem bent on destructive ends, offering a kind of critical nihilism that can only result in more fragmentation and educational disarray.

But if current criticism often seems pedagogically unrewarding, what about the literature itself that appears on the horizon? Contemporary literature can play an important part in literary education, its immediate relevance of time and place luring students into experiences that provide the basis for movement back in time, to fiction and poetry and drama of the older and more clearly classical periods. I am an enthusiastic believer in underground books, works that students find and read on their own, their act of discovery and possession becoming in itself a major stage in their literary education. My own experience in the late 1930s and early 1940s with Thomas Wolfe was determining in my own inner life. Certain recent books have provided many students with such experiences: J. D. Salinger's *Catcher in the Rye* (1951), William Golding's *Lord of the Flies* (1954), Joseph Heller's *Catch-22* (1961), Kurt Vonnegut's *Cat's Cradle* (1963). My present concern is that it has been some time now since I found my students (or heard of other students) carrying about a novel that represents personal discovery and inspires unbounded enthusiasm. My impertinent question is this: What has happened to contemporary literature?

One novelist turned critic has provided an impassioned answer to my question. In *On Moral Fiction* (1978) John Gardner sees a relationship between the obscurity of contemporary criticism and the state of contemporary art, particularly literature: "The language of critics, and of artists of the kind who pay attention to critics, has become exceedingly odd: not talk about feelings or intellectual affirmations— not talk about moving and surprising twists of plot or wonderful characters and ideas—but sentences full of large words like *hermeneutic, heuristic, structuralism, formalism,* or *opaque language,* and full of fine distinctions—for instance those between *modernist* and *post-modernist*—that would make even an intelligent cow suspicious. Though more difficult than ever before to read, criticism has become trivial." [8] These sentences are merely the warm-up for Gardner's major denunciation, which is wholesale: "In a world where nearly everything that passes for art is tinny and commercial and often, in addition, hollow and academic, I argue—by reason and by banging the table—for an old-fashioned view of what art is and does and what the fundamental business of critics ought therefore to be. Not that I want joy taken out of the arts; but even frothy entertainment is not harmed by a touch of moral responsibility, at least an evasion of too fashionable simplifications. My basic message throughout this book is as old as the hills, drawn from Homer, Plato, Aristotle, Dante, and the rest, and standard in Western civilization down through the eighteenth century. . . . The traditional view is that true art is moral: it seeks to improve life, not debase it. It seeks to hold off, at least for a while, the twilight of the gods and us. . . . That art which tends toward destruction, the art of nihilists, cynics, and merdistes, is not properly art at all. Art is essentially serious and beneficial, a game played against chaos and death, against entropy." [9]

John Gardner's words here sum up, I am sure, the feelings and thoughts of many people who have for some decades been sympathetic to new movements in the arts, and whose hopes have repeatedly turned to disappointment. In his reaction to contemporary fiction, Gardner certainly strikes a responsive chord in those like me who have had a professional and educational interest in tracking the modern American novel. It was not until I read *On Moral Fiction* that I fully realized how much I, too, had been haunted for some time by the notion that modern fiction had somehow lost its way, that it had ceased to have the kind of vital relevance to experience that I had always assumed it to have. And, indeed, my uneasy feelings were vaguely connected with moral questions that modern novels seemed to raise, directly or obliquely. But I found Gardner much more eloquent and persuasive in his denunciations than in his affirmations; and I found many of his formulations on morality as it relates to fiction disappointingly thin. It is simple in discussing morality and art, unless one makes painfully careful discriminations and qualifications, to fall into the enemy camp—the camp of the philistines who want their art to reflect and reaffirm their own comfortable and easy values. Genuinely moral art often calls into question those very values. It is a pity, therefore, that John Gardner's book was written so hastily and loosely that it might be dismissed by the serious (as it has been in many reviews) and will be misused by the superficial. But it serves the purpose of vigorously and courageously raising some hard questions that need facing.

Gardner's charges—that "our serious fiction is quite bad," that the "sickness" runs deep, reflecting an "almost total loss of faith in—or perhaps understanding of—how true art works"[10]—call to mind a prediction that Henry James made in 1900 in a short essay, "The Future of the Novel." By and large James was optimistic, emphasizing the novel's freedom from restrictions and its potentiality for achievement: the novel "can do simply everything, and that is its strength and its life. Its plasticity, its elasticity are infinite; there is no color, no extension it may not take from the nature of its subject or the temper of its craftsman." But, James noted, the novel could indeed perish, a victim of its own "superficiality" or "timidity," when it lost "a sense of what it can do."[11] Is it perhaps time to raise with Gardner the question James formulated three-quarters of a century ago: Has the novel lost the sense of what it can do? Many people have provided the answer already by ceasing to read our so-called serious fiction.

In scanning the horizon, we have seen little to give comfort. English departments are preoccupied with their own declining fortunes, criticism seems more and more to be talking to itself in an ever more private language, and literature itself, especially fiction, seems similarly self-centered and of diminishing relevance. Everyone can think of exceptions, of course, but my own personal and unscientific surveys indicate that many members of the profession are in substantial agreement. Are we witnessing a general decline of culture, in which both the humanities and the arts are giving way to the various sciences? Have we all lost faith in our profession because we have lost a "sense of what it can do"? Perhaps it is time that we turn back to the debris and the rubble and look for what might have survived.

Re-excavating the Foundations

In our panic at finding so little that is reassuring on the horizon, we might find ourselves echoing the shout, "Back to the basics." But before we let our passion to be relevant again overcome our reason, let us ask, "For what are the basics *basic*?" I assume that if I walked

down the average street of an average city in America and asked what
the basics in English were, I would find out that they were grammar,
spelling, and punctuation. And if I asked for what the basics were
basic, I would probably be told that they were basic for the important
fields of education and for life—the sciences, technology, business,
and industry. Though "back to the basics" may mean different things
to different people, by and large the slogan is aimed at reducing the
discipline of English to a large service program providing basic
literacy for individuals who can then go on with the more important
and vital subjects that are central to experience and living.

No one can be opposed to basic literacy, though many can have
genuine doubts that it can be achieved by a return to rote drill in
grammar, spelling, and punctuation. But few in the profession can
miss in the educational sloganeering of "back to the basics" a contempt for the humanities and the human and humane values to which
they are or ought to be devoted. What I would like to do now is to
exchange a temporal metaphor, "back to the basics," for a spatial
metaphor, "excavating the foundations." Instead of going back in
time, I would prefer to descend in space with my structural image to
those solid underpinnings on which the superstructure of our discipline must rest.

I have finally arrived at the term that appeared at the end of my
title, *imagination.* For those who immediately protest that the word is
vague, I reply, "Yes, it is just about as vague as the word *basics.*" But I
must insist on its use because there is no other that is so solidly a part
of the foundation of English and education in English. And I would
argue also that the word is central to human identity, to human
experience, and to human society. The aims of English may be sum-
marized as the education of the imagination. These aims place education in English as an end in itself, and not in the service of some
other, more central study or subject. In sifting through the comments
I have made on the profession during the past two decades, I find that
I have returned to the term again and again to get at what is central to
the profession, whether it be an elementary teacher reading fairy tales
to youngsters, a high school teacher directing students in a production
of *Macbeth,* a composition instructor commenting on a detailed
description of a walk through a forest preserve, a graduate professor
exploring with students the fictional theory of Henry James. All
of these activities, because they are directed at the development
and growth of the linguistic imagination, are in a radical or root
sense basic.

In supporting my argument for the imagination in the past, I have turned to two scientists for testimony regarding the reality and centrality of the imagination. In "The Biological Basis of Imagination," R. W. Gerard has written: "By such various mechanisms [the brain's billions of neurons and synapses] . . . great masses of nerve cells—the brain as a great unity—act together, and not merely do two or a billion units sum up their separate contributions, but each is part of a dynamic fluctuating activity pattern of the whole. This is the orchestra which plays thoughts of truth and beauty, which creates imagination." [12] In "The Creativeness of Life," biologist E. W. Sinnott has written: "The multiplication of man's behavioral goals and the increased complexity of his psychological patterns have enriched his mental life, but something else has been acquired during his upward progress. Gaining the power to accumulate experience and to reason was not enough to make him truly man. Another quality was necessary—the great flight of imagination. This is perhaps man's most distinctive trait, for it makes possible his creativeness." [13] To these scientific views of the nature of the imagination as it relates to creativity I wish now to add the view of a poet, Wallace Stevens: "The imagination is the power of the mind over the possibilities of things. . . . We cannot look at the past or the future except by means of the imagination. . . . [The imagination] enables us to live our own lives. We have it because we do not have enough without it. . . . The imagination is the power that enables us to perceive the normal in the abnormal, the opposite of chaos in chaos. . . . The truth seems to be that we live in concepts of the imagination before reason has established them. It may be that the imagination is a miracle of logic and that its exquisite divinations are calculations beyond analysis, as the conclusions of the reason are calculations wholly within analysis. If so, one understands perfectly that 'in the service of love and imagination nothing can be too lavish, too sublime or too festive.' " [14]

If, as scientist and poet agree, the imagination is the creative faculty, they would also agree with linguists that language is the substance and means, the vehicle and medium of the imagination. The linguistic imagination is the human miracle that remains a mystery even to an explorer of such mysteries like the revolutionary linguist Noam Chomsky. In *Language and Mind,* he writes: "Having mastered a language, one is able to understand an indefinite number of expressions that are new to one's experience . . . ; and one is able . . . to produce such expressions on an appropriate occasion, despite their novelty . . . and to be understood by others who share this still mysterious ability. The normal use of language is, in this sense, a creative activity. This creative aspect of normal language use is one fundamental factor that distinguishes human language from any known system of animal communication." With all this immense knowledge about language and the way it works, Chomsky maintains his sense of awe at its deep mystery and his respect for its centrality to the quality and nature of humanness: "When we study human language, we are approaching what some might call the 'human essence,' the distinctive qualities of mind that are, so far as we know, unique to man and that are inseparable from any critical phase of human existence, personal and social." [15]

Noam Chomsky's vision of language may be seen as complementary to the earlier views of Edward Sapir and Susanne Langer. As long ago as 1942, in *Philosophy in a New Key*, Susanne Langer rejected the reductive and highly restrictive view of language of the logical positivists and linguistic philosophers and focused on the fundamentally creative essence of language. For support she called on such scholars of language as Edward Sapir, and his formulation: "While it [language] may be looked upon as a symbolic system which reports or refers or otherwise substitutes for direct experience, it does not as a matter of actual behavior stand apart from or run parallel to direct experience but completely interpenetrates with it." [16] Sapir continues, "The purely communicative aspect of language has been exaggerated. It is best to admit that language is primarily a vocal actualization of the tendency to see realities symbolically." [17] Susanne Langer's own conception of language, fully compatible with Sapir's here, is suggested in three brief quotations. The first: "The utilitarian view of language is a mistake." The second: "The fact is that our primary world of reality *is* a verbal one." And the third: "The transformation of experience into concepts, not the elaboration of signals and symptoms, is the motive of language. Speech is through and through symbolic; and only sometimes signific. Any attempt to trace it back entirely to the needs of communication, neglecting the formulative, abstractive experience at the root of it, must land us in the sort of enigma that the problem of linguistic origins has long presented." [18]

What Gerard and Sinnott and Stevens, what Chomsky, Sapir, and Langer are driving at is what most English teachers have long known but frequently forgotten that they have known: the linguistic imagination—the faculty of the imagination and its vehicle language—is basic to human identity, existence, growth, and being. Thus the linguistic imagination is the cornerstone of that foundation we are re-excavating. On it must rest whatever structures of the profession we design. Contributing to these structures and design are all the members of our profession, from kindergarten through graduate school, all engaged in nourishing, developing, challenging, educating, the linguistic imagination of their students. Anyone so carried away by sloganeering as to misconceive that foundation as grammar, spelling, and punctuation—or some other simplistic formulation of the subject— is diminishing the profession and trivializing its purposes, capitulating to that "utilitarian view of language" rejected by Susanne Langer.

Literature in its broadest definition is the central means of education of the linguistic imagination. An English curriculum without literature is a curriculum without a soul. If an English teacher can instill a passion for reading literature in students at an early age, it is likely that those students will come naturally to know, at conscious or unconscious levels, most of the elements fundamental to growth in the other two components of the old/new English tripod—language and composition. But they will also through literature come to know much more. What it is they come to know is not, except peripherally, about literature, but about life, reality, experience, themselves and their society—and much more. And what they know they will know in ways possible by no other means. Students can be told about the transience of all things, or given statistical evidence, and they can hold the notion in their minds; but they will come to understand the meaning of transience when they fully experience John Keats's "Ode to a Nightingale," and this knowledge will settle in their bones. In literature, feeling is an important avenue to knowing, and knowing in profound ways. We might adopt Henry James's description of the ideal critic as a good definition of the ideal reader: he should be willing, even eager, "to lend himself, to project himself and steep himself, to feel and feel till he understands and to understand so well that he can say, to have perception at the pitch of passion and expression as embracing as the air, to be infinitely curious and incorrigibly patient, and yet plastic and inflammable and determinable."[19] In James's formulation for experiencing literature, feeling leads to understanding; perception and passion are inseparably intertwined. The knowledge that readers gain in reading fiction, James has said, is the knowledge of "another actual," another reality, another experience. "The vivid fable, more than anything else, gives him [the reader] this satisfaction [living the life of others] on easy terms, gives him knowledge abundant yet vicarious. It enables him to select, to take and to leave."[20]

To take and to leave. The world opens out in literature to an infinity of possibilities and choices, visions and revisions. If the linguistic imagination is stunted, the individual's being will be stunted, the inner identity and life diminished. But if that imagination is richly developed, the individual is ready to encounter life's experiences with incalculable resources invisible to the naked eye.

Literature may be seen in this way as expanding or (as James once put it) "swelling" consciousness, as extending and enlarging awareness. And in the process of the expansion and enlargement, literature provides the foundation and structure for a moral education, for the growth and development of the moral imagination. As John Gardner has reminded us in *On Moral Fiction,* literature throughout history has been considered, in its intentions and aims, moral. Only on occasion, as for example in recent times, has morality been proclaimed irrelevant to art. The subject of morality in literature is a linguistic minefield that cannot be quickly negotiated. But needless to say I am not suggesting that art is or should be didactic. What I am saying is that the artist's, and especially the literary artist's, very way of seeing the world is unavoidably, implicitly moral. Here as so often elsewhere, Henry James's cautiously worded commentary provides illumination:

> There is, I think, no more nutritive or suggestive truth . . . than that of the perfect dependence of the "moral" sense of a work of art on the amount of felt life concerned in producing it. The question comes back thus, obviously, to the kind and the degree of the artist's prime sensibility, which is the soil out of which his subject springs. The quality and capacity of that soil, its ability to "grow" with due freshness and straightness any vision of life, represents, strongly or weakly, the projected morality. . . . [But] one is far from contending that this enveloping air of the artist's humanity—which gives the last touch to the worth of the work— is not a widely and wondrously varying element; being on one occasion a rich and magnificent medium and on another a comparatively poor and ungenerous one.[21]

James's various terms associated with the moral element in literature are worth lingering over—"'moral' sense," "the artist's prime sensibility," "vision of life," "the enveloping air of the artist's humanity." And significantly, James notes that this element in literature "gives the last touch to the worth of the work." In short, this aspect of literature is basic to its nature and value. And this aspect represents a vital part of the role that literature plays in education. But it must be emphasized that good literature does not preach or moralize. It does not provide a set of rules for good conduct, nor does it provide a ready-made system of belief. Rather, it offers a world, or various worlds, for readers to enter and explore, examine and consider— through the moral imagination. Literature extends experience, enlarges possibility, and liberates reader-participants from the narrow range of their own moral parochialism and prejudices. And readers are thus provided the choices in wide variety through contemplation of which they may find their own moral sense and identity grow and mature.

I cannot conceive of anything more basic to our profession than the imagination, nor any more fundamental aim for us and for society than its education. We must not be deflected from this aim by a movement back to "basics" that are in reality peripheral or even trivial. This is not to say that grammar, spelling, and punctuation—and much more of related nature—cannot find a proper place in the curriculum, but in a subordinate, not a basic, position. Nor is this to say that study of some aspects of our subject might not be designed to be useful in helping a student get a job or become a doctor or lawyer. But if in devoting our attention to these parts of our profession we begin to see our discipline as in essence a service discipline without its own solid base and self-sufficient, vital purposes and ends, then we shall indeed be lost. We shall one day in the future find ourselves sifting through the debris and digging for the foundations and discover that, through our own neglect, they have crumbled away beneath us.

Notes

1. *The Uses of English: Guides for the Teaching of English from the Anglo-American Conference at Dartmouth College* (New York: Holt, Rinehart and Winston, 1967); *Growth through English* (New York: Modern Language Association of America, 1967).

2. "The Linguistic Imagination," *College English* 31 (April 1970): 725.

3. Northrop Frye, "The Archetypes of Literature," in *Myth and Method: Modern Theories of Fiction*, ed. James E. Miller, Jr. (Lincoln: University of Nebraska Press, 1960), p. 144.

4. Harold Bloom, *Wallace Stevens: The Poems of Our Climate* (Ithaca: Cornell University Press, 1977), pp. 375-406.

5. Harold Bloom, *The Anxiety of Influence: A Theory of Poetry* (New York: Oxford University Press, 1973), pp. 14-16.

6. Ibid., p. 154.

7. Ibid., pp. 94-95.

8. John Gardner, *On Moral Fiction* (New York: Basic Books, 1978), p. 4.

9. Ibid., pp. 5-6.

10. Ibid., p. 100.

11. Henry James, *Theory of Fiction: Henry James*, ed. James E. Miller, Jr. (Lincoln: University of Nebraska Press, 1972), p. 340.

12. R. W. Gerard, "The Biological Basis of Imagination," *Scientific Monthly* 62 (1946): 477-99.

13. E. W. Sinnott, "The Creativeness of Life," in *Creativity*, ed. B. E. Vernon (Harmondsworth, Middlesex: Penguin Books, 1970), p. 108.

14. Wallace Stevens, "Imagination as Value," in *The Necessary Angel* (New York: Random House, Vintage Books, 1965), pp. 133–56.

15. Noam Chomsky, *Language and Mind* (New York: Harcourt, Brace and World, 1968; enlarged edition, 1972), p. 100.

16. Edward Sapir, "Language," in *Culture, Language and Personality: Selected Essays*, ed. David G. Mandelbaum (Berkeley: University of California Press, 1970), p. 8.

17. Sapir, p. 15.

18. Susanne K. Langer, *Philosophy in a New Key: A Study in the Symbolism of Reason, Rite, and Art*, 2d ed. (New York: New American Library, Mentor, 1951), pp. 107 and 113.

19. James, pp. 331–32.

20. Ibid., p. 338.

21. Ibid., p. 313.

The Unconscious at Work in Reading

Bruno Bettelheim
Professor Emeritus, University of Chicago

Reading, from the very beginning, can be a process in which one is actively and in very personal ways involved, or it can be an essentially passive procedure in which large and important segments of the personality remain unengaged, or may even resist the process. That is, learning to read can either involve all of our personality, including its deepest layers, or it can be a process in which only our cognitive capacities participate in decoding, while the rest of our personality remains essentially untouched. Reading—the process of extracting meaning from what is printed on the page—is an active cognitive process, but as long as we take in only what the text tries to convey, we permit ourselves to be passively impressed by what somebody else wishes to impress upon us. Only if we reshape the content in accordance with our preoccupations, if we pour ourselves into the act of reading and actively recreate—to some degree in our image—what we are reading, does the content become vitally important to us, and with it reading in general. In the first case reading is and remains a task which has to be met; in the second, reading becomes something to which we are deeply and most personally committed—it becomes literacy.

One significant element at work here is the share the unconscious plays in shaping the process of appreciating a work of art or literature. So far this role of the unconscious has received little attention, although its investigation would open vistas of great consequence for our understanding of why some persons derive great benefit from reading good literature while others remain indifferent to it. Compared to study of the role of cognition in reading and that of a reader's conscious responses to a piece of literature, examination of unconscious reactions lags far behind. What goes on in the unconscious, however, significantly shapes the reader's responses to any work. In fact, the overt and covert messages contained in what a person is reading often arouse unconscious reactions that are quite at variance with what the author had intended.

This is true in general, even when a reader happens not to be engaged in a very personal way with what he or she is reading. If a reader is so engaged, then personal concerns intrude into the content, and they do more so as the reader becomes more emotionally involved. How far astray idiosyncratic reactions to a text will carry a reader depends to a considerable degree on the reader's ability to think abstractly, and on his or her experience in doing so. The less intellectually sophisticated the reader, the less he or she is accustomed to comprehending matters in accordance with abstract reasoning and the more he or she is apt to be swayed by emotions or the mood of the moment, thus distorting the meaning of what is being read in line with the feelings the material arouses.

Our understanding of the processes at work in us that account for the disparity between messages intended by an author and meanings received by a particular reader is limited, but it is incomparably more advanced than our comprehension of the unconscious forces within us that condition our responses to a piece of literature when we try not just to comprehend it but also, for some reason of our own, want to make it part of our personal experience. And we know even less of what is involved when conscious and unconscious preoccupations intrude on the comprehension and appreciation of what we are reading to the degree that we read differently from the printed text, or when we become resistant—or in extreme cases unable—to read parts or all of it.

The younger and the less intellectually mature readers are, the more powerfully do their emotions assert themselves in all they do, and the less able are they to experience things abstractively and objectively—even less are young readers able to prevent their unconscious from obtruding and distorting what they are consciously trying to comprehend. These are well-known facts, but in the teaching of reading to beginners, these facts are largely neglected! The unconscious is not even mentioned in the most highly regarded and widely used treatises on the teaching of reading today. But in the beginning reader who is a young child, that which originates in the inner mental life conditions responses to what is read much more than does the content of the text.

While the young child may occasionally engage in quiet contemplation, the natural tendency is to prefer active manipulation. So the basic texts from which the young reader is taught describe children engaging in various activities: running, playing ball, riding bikes. The error here is that reading about activities is a far cry from engaging in them; in many ways sitting quietly while reading about such activities makes the child wish to do them instead of reading about them. This makes reading less attractive than it would be had the child's mind not been incited to think about being active.

While a reader is cognitively active while trying to comprehend the message contained in what is being read, he or she is nevertheless to a large degree also passively receptive to what the text attempts to convey. By contrast, if the reader in some measure deviates from the text to reshape spontaneously the intended message, making it more congenial to what consciously or unconsciously preoccupies his or her mind at the moment, trying to bring it more in line with past experiences and present concerns, the reader is actively manipulating the text's meaning as he or she deviates from it. Without being consciously aware of that deviation, the reader actively modifies that which otherwise would be passively taken in. This makes the text much more personally important to the reader, giving the specific piece a personal imprint, and indirectly making reading in general more important. Compared to such active dealing with reading, efforts at trying to get exactly what the text tries to convey are passive and receptive and in most cases rather uninteresting.

This is common knowledge. It is the reason why the so-called stories of basic readers present topics thought to be personally attractive and meaningful to children of the age at which most are introduced to reading. The psychological error here, of course, is that although an activity may be attractive to a child, reading about it in oversimplified form frequently is not. For example, just because first-graders are familiar with the complex personal interactions in a ball game and their emotions are aroused by the ebb and flow of the fortunes of their team does not mean that a text that tries to describe the game with an extremely limited vocabulary will be of high interest to first-graders. Being reminded by the text of ball games may induce children to think about them, but it will also convince them that reading about ball games is trite indeed when compared with the vital events of a real game. The result will be that children learn that reading is not worth the effort involved because all it can offer is a mean picture of that with which it deals.

Watching first- or second-graders laboriously struggling to make sense of their readers shows that all they are involved in is trying to decode words correctly; the content of what they are reading seldom has much potential personal meaning to them, and in most cases no actual meaning whatsoever. As much time as beginning readers spend on figuring out the text—and often considerably more—they devote to workbooks. From them no meaning, personal or otherwise, can be extracted. Workbooks merely require decoding for decoding's sake.

Teachers, too, concentrate on giving help in decoding and on correcting decoding errors. True, after a piece of reading has been completed—and sometimes in anticipation of its being read—teachers try to arouse the children's interest in the material, but this encouragement rarely succeeds in infusing the act of reading with personal significance for too much of the child's labor and energy has gone into the act of decoding, and the text's content is too trivial. The energy expended on decoding and the discouraging defeats many children experience when trying to decode, combined with essentially uninteresting content, prevent them from getting excited about the text; reading as such is, therefore, a tedious, unrewarding task.

Often children do become personally involved in the subjects they and their teachers talk about, since many teachers are able to make conversations about the content of a text interesting. But the comparison between the text and the conversation makes the text appear in an even worse light: it conveys so little of what could have been said about the topic as shown by the conversation with the teacher. Unfortunately, positive experiences between teacher and child center on personal interactions and do not affect the child's feelings about decoding or reading in general. The teacher's remarks may help a child to understand the material that has been read, but the moment for deep personal commitment to reading has passed.

Perhaps I can make my point with this example. We have all had the experience of reading a poem the merits of which we recognized, but which nevertheless failed to impress or move us in any personal way. Then an expert explains the poem to us; the poem now appears much more meaningful; we comprehend what the poet was about in writing it and understand what others have gained from it. Valuable as all this is, and much as it may help us later in our appreciation of the poem, there is no personal delight in the poem and no shock of recognition such as we might have experienced if our response had been spontaneous. This remains so until we reread the poem, but now with much deeper feeling for its music, its poetic appeal, its mood, the meaning of its symbols. The difference between the two readings is that while we passively took the poem in the first time, we actively make it our own the second time.

The difficulty with my example, however, is that the texts from which beginners are taught to read have little intrinsic value. What they convey does not grow on children with rereading. Teachers are so much aware of this that I have never observed them suggesting that children reread those texts. Nor have I seen children spontaneously re-reading them after the teacher's discussion of their content.

It is true that material not personally meaningful at one time may become so later on, and we teach children to read in the hope that what they read in the future will have meaning for them. But I submit that a skill that was not intrinsically meaningful when we learned it, an activity that was devoid of meaning during the first years we engaged in it, is much less likely to become deeply meaningful later on compared with activities that captivated the deepest layers of our being from the very beginning. Reading as we teach it is the acquisition of a skill; our teaching neither creates an inner attitude towards reading favorable to becoming literate, nor does it convey knowledge that the child cherishes.

Reading texts, because of their limited and controlled vocabulary, contain nothing that is new to children and rarely anything of inherent interest to them. Even if it were possible truly to interest children in the content of texts, the vocabulary used in them and the level of thought are so far below those which children engage in all on their own that the texts in effect talk down to them. All these are reasons why it is impossible for children to involve themselves personally in the act of reading, unless they do so for reasons extraneous to the process of being taught to read.

It is well known how easily children learn to read when their motivation to do so is derived from their home experiences, and many children come to school already motivated to learn to read. But these are children who, at the right time, would teach themselves to read; they pose no problems. Their example shows that when children out of very personal reasons want to become actively involved in reading, they will do so.

Again, it ought to be stressed that beginning readers are not at a developmental age when they are prone to passive contemplation. Instead, their active, manipulative tendencies are at the highest, and they are eager to make things their very own by giving them a personal imprint. We all are much more deeply committed to what we actively shape or reshape than we are to what we accept as offered; and this is more true for the young child than it is for the adult. Thus, whether children develop a deep and lasting commitment to reading is strongly influenced by whether they view reading as something imposed on them from the outside, or as something they help to create.

It is a strange fact that in teaching reading to beginners we discourage their active manipulation of what is read; instead, we insist that children should be cognitively active in reading words as printed but emotionally passive. In short, they are forbidden to reshape what they read in line with what is most important to them—that which goes on in their innermost lives. By such insistence we deprive learning to read of much that makes it most attractive to children. We involve only their cognitive capacities in the process of learning to read, and we exclude their unconscious life from participating in it. It stands to reason that we would be much more successful in fostering deep commitment to reading if from the very beginning we involved the child's total personality in the process of reading.

All this was brought forcefully to my attention during many years of working with severely disturbed children at the University of Chicago's Orthogenic School. Only by taking cognizance of how the child's unconscious was involved in reading, or often in the refusal to learn to read, were we able to induce nonreaders to learn to read, and to make reading attractive to children who had determinedly refused to be interested in it. By appealing to the unconscious of these children we succeeded in making reading not just possible, but desirable for nonreaders, many of whom later became avid readers. Often we discovered that these children were nonreaders because the manner in which they had personalized what they read had been completely unacceptable to their teachers and other adults. Only as we made it possible for them to imbue reading again—or for the first time—with important personal meaning did they become readers, and readers who now knew that reading could provide them with personal experiences full of deepest meaning. A few examples may illustrate.

One girl claimed to be completely unable to recognize letters, not to mention being unable to read. Eventually she let on that her inability to read originated in her ability to do so. Her name was Leslie. At an early age this supposed nonreader had realized that the second syllable of her name read *lie*. Circumstances had forced her to create and live in a world of lies so that she would not be destroyed by inimical forces in whose powers she was, or at least felt to be. Her life seemed an impenetrable web of lies, so she decided to have nothing to do with letters that so clearly revealed this in the last syllable of her name.

Only after she had been helped to recognize that it was not so much that she, Leslie, wanted to be a liar, but rather that those in whose power she felt to be had lied to her, and had forced her to lie in return for safety's sake, did she become able and willing to recognize her name. But she insisted that it was to be spelled *Lieslie* because her existence had been nothing but a heaping of lies on top of the basic lie that she had felt forced to pretend to like a parent, although she had lived in mortal fear of this parent. In a later development, when she was able to relinquish most of her pretend life and to see herself less as a complete liar, she spontaneously insisted that her name was to be spelled *Lesslie,* for she was not living *less* of a *lie*. At this time she became willing to learn to read.

All along this girl's name had had deepest personal meaning for her, as names have for many children. Because we accepted the spelling of her name as Lesslie, and because this word was of such unique importance to her, she began to accept that other words, and with it reading, had things of personal significance to offer her. On this basis reading eventually became important to her. It was difficult for her to give up lying altogether as the basis of safety in her life, and only when she achieved a sufficiently strong feeling of security, and with it respect for herself, was she able to spell and read her name as Leslie. Since we had reacted positively to her various idiosyncratic spellings of her name, she could finally make her own the common spelling of her name, and with this accept the spelling of all other words.

Another child acted as if she were feebleminded. With great determination she refused to be involved in any learning task. She, too, had had a most unfortunate early history. She had been severely abused by her parents and in consequence had been placed in various foster homes, none of which had worked out because of her extreme negativism. At the Orthogenic School, because of her teacher's ability to befriend her, the child was willing to go to class, occupying herself there with all sorts of things, provided no learning whatsoever was involved. But being in class, she could not help hearing what went on around her as some children learned to read.

One day when some of the other children were reading stories about happy families, stories that described good relations between parents and children, how they played together and talked, the teacher sat down beside the girl and spoke with her about how upsetting it must be for her to hear all these stories about good homes when her experiences with homes had been so very bad. Using the child's customary language, the teacher observed that it was high time to teach a lesson to the people who write such stories and expect children to learn to read from them. The teacher suggested that the girl might like to correct such a story (a simple reading text of some forty pages with only a limited number of words on each page) by taking parents out of the stories by blotting out with a heavy black marker the words *father* and *mother* whenever they appeared.

The girl seemed completely uninterested in this suggestion, but the teacher, undaunted, proceeded with her own marker to blot out these words on the first three pages. By the fourth page the girl appeared interested and amused. The teacher went on a little longer and by the sixth page asked the girl whether she would like to continue doing the same thing throughout the book. This nonreader, who could not recognize a single word—or so she maintained—now systematically and faultlessly blotted out *father* and *mother* on the following thirty-odd pages. When the child had as if through "magic" manipulation of words made the book fit her psychological needs, the teacher asked her whether she might now try to read the book, for her an advanced text in view of her supposedly nonexistant reading ability. The girl read it with scarcely an error.

Some might argue that it would have been better to let the child dictate her own story in order to learn to read from it—but this had been tried without success. Requests to do something positive, such as dictating a story, had proved fruitless because the bad in the girl's life had blotted out the good. Only after she became active in the manipulation of the reading material did reading attain meaning for her, and then it was fairly easily mastered. Unhappy means sometimes serve happy ends, but happy learning experiences are always achieved when the cognitive efforts of young children are supported by their unconscious needs. It is the reshaping of what is read in accord with their most pressing needs that makes reading irresistibly attractive to children.

The preceding examples illustrate how nonreaders can become readers when they are enabled to personalize their reading in ways that make the experience deeply significant, a significance that then spreads to reading in general. A quite different example may show that if a child, all on his or her own, manages to personalize a reading experience and to hold on to that experience, despite the most severe psychological disturbance, that child may remain or become an excellent reader.

In a different context I discussed the case of Dana, a catatonic, anorexic, schizophrenic girl.[1] Despite her catatonic frozenness and completely irresponsive attitude to the world, she had remained a good student and interested in reading. After years of treatment she finally revealed why: one word in particular had been endowed with the deepest personal meaning, and this word was so tremendously important to her that she had become and remained interested in words, and reading in general. The word that had such personal meaning to her was *weather*. Although incapacitated by the anxiety that she might be devoured and destroyed by her mother and by other persons whom she endowed with similar destructive powers, this child had decided that the secret intentions of her enemies would be revealed to her by the seemingly innocuous word *weather*, since it contained in hidden form the message *we eat her*. Fascination with one word and its meanings had permitted her to become and remain a good reader. Freed of her anxieties, she was able to extend this fascination to serious reading, which became a main interest in her life.

The positive responses of disturbed children to the opportunity to reshape what they read in accord with their highly idiosyncratic needs suggest that normal children, too, might become more personally involved in reading when their active reshaping of what they read is not criticized or rejected as error but accepted positively. We decided to test this hypothesis in a number of classrooms.[2] We found not only that acceptance of the personalization of reading by beginners, as we had expected, led to more positive attitudes towards reading in general but also, much to our surprise, that treating such so-called errors as meaningful and purposeful resulted in the vast majority of cases in their immediate and spontaneous correction—and this without our having in any way pointed out to the children that something had been amiss.

An eight-and-a-half-year-old boy was not doing well enough academically, since he learned more slowly than had his sisters with whom he was often disparagingly compared. One day he was struggling with a Walt Disney version of *Cinderella* and had reached the part of the story where stepmother and stepsisters do not permit Cinderella time off from her labors to prepare herself for the ball. They mock her: "You must learn to work faster." Finally, she is able to put on her dress: "Cinderella ran down the stairs. 'Wait,' she called, 'I can go now.'" Instead of reading the words as printed, the boy read: "Cinderella ran down the *sisters*," and then he stopped. As if the sentence had been unfinished, we concluded it by adding "because she was so mad." At that, he spontaneously reread the line exactly as printed.

This boy felt pushed to work better, that is, faster in school, so he identified with Cinderella. While the Cinderella story does not say that she was angry at being made so little of, we feel she must have been. The boy in his misreading made her give vent to her anger—and his—in an aggressive act directed against those who behave in such superior fashion. Our giving words to Cinderella's anger—and with it, implicitly, to his—conveyed to the boy that we understood why he had read the sentence the way he did, and that we accepted as valid the feelings he had expressed in his misreading. Through it he had put into words his desire to "run down" those who push children to work faster than they can or want to do. Stating the wish to get even probably provided some relief for this boy; our acceptance of his anger in a matter of fact way did the rest. Unconscious pressure from inner rage was reduced sufficiently so that it no longer interfered with the cognitive task of reading the words as printed, a task which the boy could now attend to. All this was clear demonstration that his misreading had not been due to lack of reading skill.

Had we corrected his error in reading, as his teacher typically did, his anger and his frustration with himself would have increased. We would have fueled his wish to "run down" those who pressed him to read faster, and better, and would have made it much more difficult for him to read the sentence as it was written. Criticism of his attempt to express what the text had aroused in him would have reminded him of past criticisms from parents and teachers, and this reminder might have increased his anger to such a degree that it would have overwhelmed his cognitive powers. Asked to read what was printed, the boy probably would have blocked, as he was wont to do in similar situations. He might have stopped reading altogether, claiming that he could not do it. The reason would have been that the overwhelming pressure of his emotions would have "blinded" him, so to speak, making it impossible for him to recognize words not in line with his feelings.

It would be a mistake to assume that through his correct second reading of the sentence the boy had rewarded us for having taken his side in his conflict with those who pressed him to "work," to learn faster than he could; that to please us he had read the text as it was written. While our relationship may have played a small part in his spontaneous correction, much more important in the long run is that he pleased himself by successfully mastering the cognitive task presented by the text. That he was able to do so all on his own, without prodding or help from us—such as asking him to take another look at the word, to sound it out, to consider whether nice Cinderella would do such a nasty thing, all interventions teachers typically use in attempting to help children correct themselves—demonstrated to the boy that he could read correctly, that his misreading was not due to incompetence, a conclusion that is inescapable if somebody points out an error before one can correct oneself. Such pleasure in oneself and in one's achievement extends backward to the process of reading, because it was the experience of reading that led to it.

The boy's first misreading had invested the text with deep personal meaning for him. The correct second reading provided the experience of pleasure in himself, and with it in reading. It is experiences such as these that eventually lead to literacy, based on the conviction that reading is both meaningful and personally satisfying.

Such was the desirable consequence of accepting a misreading as meaningful, albeit not as one that corresponded to the printed text. Quite different results might have come from correcting the boy's misreading. An attentive teacher might have pointed out that the word in the text did indeed begin with the letter *s*, but that it was not *sisters*. That teacher would have been following what she or he had learned about common mistakes in reading: when two words begin with the same letter, as *sisters* and *stairs* do, beginning readers may make a mistake because they decode correctly the first letter and then guess at the rest of the word. This theory completely disregards what was in truth going on in the boy's mind, which was worlds apart from guessing a word, since he was projecting important personal meaning into the story. Such a correction, by denying validity to what was going on in the boy's mind and by making him appear as less competent than he was, would certainly have aroused negative feelings. Even if he had corrected himself at such prompting, his action would have been yet another demonstration—to himself, to his teacher, and to other students—of his shortcomings. We hate that which makes us look incompetent in the eyes of others and feel incompetent in our own eyes. Such resentment extends backwards, too, to what caused such exasperating feelings, in this example to reading, and to all it stands for.

This negative extension is exactly what happens in every beginners' class, every school day, as the most casual observation of the teaching of reading readily shows. True, it does not happen to each child every day, but it does happen to children as part of the reading experience because they are exposed at least several times each day to the teacher's corrections of the misreadings of other children. Of course children do not consciously understand the psychological ramifications of what is going on, but subconsciously the experience nevertheless makes a deep impression because it was not so long ago that they had been the ones who had made similar errors in reading by expressing their inner feelings, and the teacher's critical behavior had demonstrated that what was truly important to them—the meaning they had found in the story—had no place in reading. The serious impact of such experiences is further aggravated by the insecurity of beginning readers, which makes correction particularly painful. And the pain is even greater because children know that how they read the text was the right way because it corresponded to what was going on in their minds. Nevertheless, they are forced by the authority of the teacher to agree that their reading was not correct, and this admission makes them feel incompetent.

The worst aspect of all this is the monstrous degree to which teacher and child are at cross purposes. Learning to read, and even more important, to enjoy reading, requires most of all that the teacher's purposes in teaching a child to read and the child's purposes in learning to read be identical. The teacher, unfortunately, is convinced that correction of misreading makes the story more meaningful to the child, while in fact it robs the story of all personal meaning for the child. The teacher believes that correction makes reading attractive, but from the child's point of view, correction spoils the pleasure to be gained from reading.

This example also shows that the positive acceptance of a child's misreading as meaningful in terms of what makes a story significant to the reader can lead to—and most often does lead to—a second reading of the text as printed—and this without bringing the misreading to the child's attention. All this is in line with the developmental stage of the young reader, which is one of transition from idiosyncratic to abstract thought. Having first experienced appreciation of a highly personalized reading of a story, the child is able to move on to a more objective acceptance of the story's content.

Teachers of normal youngsters can help to change reading from something children try to avoid into something that they find fascinating and highly rewarding by accepting and approving of the unconscious reactions of youngsters to reading. What had appeared to them as a tedious, sometimes impossible task, since they blocked completely while trying to read, becomes an exciting experience when teachers give recognition to the unconscious reason for such blocking, and with that recognition a connection is established between conscious efforts at decoding and unconscious inability to do so. In short, conscious and unconscious reactions to reading are brought to bear on each other.

An energetic, assertive, almost pugnacious boy was reading a story about two children fighting. He blocked on the word *fight*, pronouncing only the *f* sound, unable to go on. The teacher tried to help him sound out the word—in fact, was pleased that he had sounded out the initial letter. The boy continued to block. She defined the word for him, all to no avail; he became only more stubbornly resistant. However, when she began to talk about the content of the story, how typical fighting is among children, how adults ought to understand the child's need for it, the boy suddenly could read the word, and told, somewhat sheepishly, how he and his sister frequently fought. The boy had not substituted another word for the word *fight* because he could think of no compromise between his need to fight and his anxiety about it.

Blocking on the word *fight* was clear indication that the boy had subconsciously read the word correctly; otherwise, the blocking would not have begun with this word. Sounding out the first letter—as in many similar cases—is tantamount to a statement from the child: "It is not lack of intellectual ability that makes it impossible for me to read this word, but emotional blocking. If it were not knowing the letters, I would not know even the first letter. Knowing the first letter would facilitate reading the word, if the problem were one of knowing letters." When the teacher showed that she understood the boy's dilemma by talking about the associations the word *fight* evoked in his mind, he could read it. Her remarks about how common it is for boys of his age to fight had helped him to understand that his subconscious feeling that it was wrong for him to think about fighting, the emotion that had blocked him, was not what the text had wished to convey, or at least not what his teacher thought. This perception permitted him to understand that what had blocked him was not the content of the story but his feelings that it was very wrong for him to fight with his sister.

My purpose in drawing attention to the unconscious phenomena that account for blockings and misreadings was not that their consideration permits the spontaneous removal of a reading block or the correction of a misreading, although these are often the desirable consequences. My intention was to suggest that treating the unconscious aspects in reading with respect in accordance with the important concerns of the reading child which they reflect changes reading that before seemed an arduous chore into an exciting and enlightening experience. Reading that had been viewed as a much too difficult and boring experience then becomes endowed with deep meaning and for that reason is sought by the child with enthusiasm.

Notes

1. *A Home for the Heart* (New York: Alfred A. Knopf, 1974).

2. The following data were collected as part of research made possible by a grant from the Spencer Foundation, whose support is gratefully acknowledged. A publication on this investigation has been prepared by the two main investigators, Karen Zelan and the author of this paper, *On Learning to Read: The Child's Fascination with Meaning* (New York: Alfred A. Knopf, 1981).

Contributors

Bruno Bettelheim, Distinguished Professor of Education Emeritus and Professor Emeritus of both psychology and psychiatry at the University of Chicago, is the author of many volumes in child psychology. Among them are *The Informed Heart* and *Love Is Not Enough.* In 1977 he won the National Book Award and the National Book Critics' Circle Award for *The Uses of Enchantment.* His most recent publication, with Karen Zelan, is *On Learning to Read: The Child's Fascination with Meaning.*

Wayne C. Booth, Professor of English at the University of Chicago, has been a Ford Faculty, Guggenheim, and Rockefeller Foundation Fellow and a visiting lecturer at Princeton, Indiana University, and the University of California at Berkeley and at Irvine. Among his works are *The Rhetoric of Fiction,* for which he won the Christian Gauss Award of Phi Beta Kappa and the David H. Russell Award of the National Council of Teachers of English, *A Rhetoric of Irony,* and *Critical Understanding: The Powers and Limits of Pluralism.*

George Hillocks, Jr., teaches in the Departments of Education and English at the University of Chicago. In addition to numerous journal articles, he has written *Alternatives in English: A Critical Appraisal of Elective Programs* and *Observing and Writing* and is coauthor of *Dynamics of English Instruction.*

E. D. Hirsch, Jr., teaches at the University of Virginia and has served as the chair of its Department of English and as Director of Composition. He has been a Fulbright fellow, a Guggenheim fellow, and a fellow with the National Endowment for the Humanities. Among his books are *Innocence and Experience: An Introduction to Blake,* for which he received the *Explicator* award, *Validity in Interpretation,* and *The Philosophy of Composition.*

James E. Miller, Jr., has served the National Council of Teachers of English as president, as trustee of the Research Foundation, as director of the Commission on Literature, and as editor of *College English.* Currently at the University of Chicago, he has taught at Northwestern University, at the University of Nebraska, and at the University of Hawaii and held Fulbright lectureships in Italy and Japan. Among his books are studies of Whitman, Melville, and F. Scott Fitzgerald, *Quests Surd and Absurd: Essays in American Literature,* and *Word, Self, and Reality: The Rhetoric* *of Imagination.* In 1975 Professor Miller received the Distinguished Service Award of the National Council of Teachers of English.

James R. Squire, Senior Vice-President with Ginn and Company, served the National Council of Teachers of English as Executive Secretary from 1960–67. Coauthor of *The Teaching of Language and Literature* and *The National Interest and the Teaching of English,* he has published in many professional journals and lectured at colleges and universities and professional meetings throughout the country.

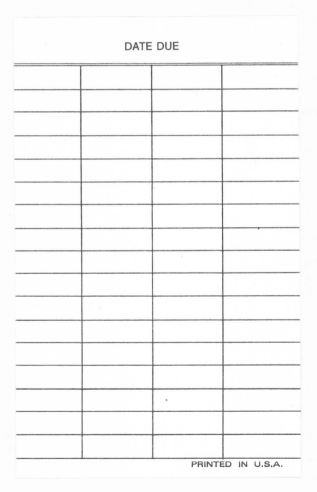

DATE DUE

PRINTED IN U.S.A.